Hometown Sports Heroes Vol. 1

16 Classic Baseball Tales

By: Mike Hauser

Great Point Publishing

Gloversville, NY

Hometown Sports Heroes, Vol. 1: 16 Classic Baseball Tales
By: Mike Hauser

Cover Design By: Gareth Bobowski

Book design by: Great Point Publishing LLC

To order additional copies of this title, contact your favorite local bookstore or visit *www.greatpointpublishing.com*

Paperback ISBN: 978-1-7333797-2-4

Printed in the United States of America

Published by: **Great Point Publishing, LLC.**
Gloversville, NY

Dedicated to my biggest critics and my biggest fans; my parents, Tom & Karen Hauser.

Thank you for being such great role models and always pushing me to be better than I was content with being!

Table of Contents

Introduction

The Rarest Diamond in the World   i
    By: Christopher Hallenbeck

Hometown Sports Heroes, Vol. 1: 16 Classic Baseball Tales

Russell Holmes- Gloversville's Fenway Park Connection   1

Grimshaw brings the big leagues, Cy Young to Gloversville   9

Schumacher – Upstate New York's Prince of Baseball   18

Chickens, Tigers, & Pirates... Mayfield Baseball of course   26

Jack McKeon... Back to his Gloversville Roots   36

Pittsburgh Pirates once visited Gloversville's Berkshire Park   44

The Integration of Professional Baseball... in Fulton County   50

110th Anniversary of the Greatest Month in Gloversville Baseball   59

Vintage Baseball in Fulton County   66

Generations mirror each other at Parkhurst Field   70

Foster, Sanford... Baseball with a Flair   76

The Death and Rebirth of an economy at the Ballpark   86

70th Anniversary of Fredericks' season with the Glovers   91

Musillo joins Hall of Fame   98

Baseball's Clown Prince appears in Gloversville   105

The Undefeated GHS Maroon Nine...   109

About the Author   120

A Note from Mike...   121

Also by Mike...   121

End Notes   122

The Rarest Diamond in the World
By: Christopher Hallenbeck

On the night of May 21, 1885, Victor Hugo wrote in his diary: "Nothing, not all the armies of the world, can stop an idea whose time has come." The following day, Victor Hugo, a man who was considered one of the greatest and best-known French writers, a writer whose most famous works included the novels _Les Misérables_ and _The Hunchback of Notre-Dame_, passed away at the age of 83.[1,2]

Hometown Sports Heroes, Vol. 1, by Mike Hauser features a collection of short stories and shortstops, both playing the position of defense, helping make sure these classic baseball tales are not lost to time and forgotten memories. While reading Hauser's classic baseball tales, you will notice that, in some of the stories, you're going to read about a baseball park called "A., J. & G Park"/ "Parkhurst Field".

"A., J. & G Park"/ "Parkhurst Field" is mentioned many times in this book because so many baseball cleats have dug into the dirt there for over 100 years. Countless eyes have captured moments that were originally shared by word of mouth, and those memories are now shared through Mike Hauser's efforts to your eyes. The story of "A., J. & G Park"/ "Parkhurst Field" begins on July 12, 1906. This is the story of the rarest diamond in the world.

On July 12, 1906, 21 years after Victor Hugo's passing, the F, J & G Railroad Company opened a new baseball park on Harrison Street in Gloversville, N.Y.

The new venue was named "A., J. & G Park" and it was to be the home of the professional New York State League's JAGs (Johnstown-Amsterdam-Gloversville), a baseball team that was formed, and owned, by the Railroad Company four years earlier in 1902. [3, 4, 5]

A Gloversville architect, F.L. Comstock, designed "A., J. & G Park", and E.A. Satterlee built it for $3,088 on six acres of land that was leased from C.W. Judson on Harrison Street. The ballpark was located midway between Gloversville and Johnstown, N.Y., on a field near where the train would run past. As part of the designs for

"A., J. & G Park", the architects featured a grandstand that accommodated 1,500 spectators, and the baseball clubhouse at "A., J. & G Park" was patterned after one of the best clubhouses in The National League.[3, 6]

A Gloversville man, Sam Lucas, constructed the baseball diamond, utilizing a new type of drainage system, so the field could be used within a short time after a storm. The diamond was also arranged so that the sun would not shine directly in the eyes of the outfielders.[7,8]

Mr. Lucas was 30 years old when he built the baseball diamond for "A., J. & G Park", and because of the excellence and reputation of his work there, Mr. Lucas was given contracts for the construction of baseball diamonds in Elmira, Wilkes-Barre, and Utica. Mr. Lucas' talents were also recognized and sought out on a national level, as he also later built the grounds at Forbes Field in Pittsburgh in 1909 and was asked to take charge of the N.Y. Giants Polo Grounds. A number of other teams also sought his services as a groundskeeper; however, he decided to return home to Gloversville. At the time of Mr. Lucas' passing in 1971, "A., J. & G Park" was still considered one of the best baseball diamonds in modern times. [3, 7]

In <u>Hometown Sports Heroes</u>, Vol. 1, author Mike Hauser writes,

> *"Based on the success of attendance during the 1906 season, and a professional field that rivaled that of any Major League park at that time. The F., J. & G. Railroad (owners of the JAGS) decided to begin booking Major League Teams who were traveling through the Mohawk Valley in route from games in Boston, going to Major League cities out West. Additional game ticket sales and train fare from fans to get to the park were the motivators. Such exhibition game detours on off/travel days also served as a means for the Major League team owners to help defray the costs of their road trips. Team train fare, hotels and meal costs were recouped as the Big-League clubs received a lump sum appearance fee and/or a percentage of the gate receipts."* [4]

Essentially, by contacting Major League teams, the owners of The F., J., & G. Railroad (and "A., J. & G Park") were unknowingly utilizing a future marketing strategy, called *Positioning*.

Positioning, was introduced by Jack Trout in 1969, and the concept was later expanded upon in the marketing classic, <u>Positioning: The Battle for Your Mind</u>, by Al Ries and Jack Trout. In short, *"Positioning is thinking in reverse. Instead of starting with yourself, you start with the mind of your prospect."* [2, 10]

This marketing technique would become highly successful for the owners of "A., J. & G Park" beginning with the 1907 baseball season.

In <u>Hometown Sports Heroes</u>, Vol. 1, Hauser writes,

> *"On July 5, 1907 while on route from Boston to Detroit to play the Tigers, Moose Grimshaw and the entire Boston (Red Sox) Americans team stopped in Gloversville to play an exhibition game. The game took place at A., J. & G Park against the JAGS team... Because of the proximity to Grimshaw's hometown, the team made the stop to play the game knowing that lots of Grimshaw's family & friends from the Mohawk Valley would make the trip to see the game. 11 days later, on Tuesday July 16, 1907, the Scranton Miners came to A., J. & G Park to play a New York State League game against the JAGS. With this team was a 29-year-old player by the name of Archibald "Moonlight Doc" Graham. Graham played left field. Graham was the subject of the 1989 Universal Pictures blockbuster baseball drama called "Field of Dreams". 8 days after 'Moonlight' Graham and the Scranton Miners played in Gloversville, the Pittsburgh Nationals (now Pirates) arrived at A., J. & G Park to play against the JAGS in an exhibition game on July 24, 1907. Playing in that game for the Pittsburgh Nationals was their shortstop, and now baseball legend and Hall of Famer, named Honus Wagner."* [4, 11]

These types of exhibition games would become a major part of baseball history and are known today as Barnstorming Baseball. The National Baseball Hall of Fame writes, *"These 'barnstorming' tours played an important role in the development of the National Pastime..."* [9]

In 1918, the F.J.&G Railroad Company gave up their lease on the "A., J. & G Park" property, and the Parkhurst family purchased the baseball grounds. Because of this transaction, "A., J. & G Park" was now called "Parkhurst Field", and for the next thirty years, "Parkhurst Field" continued to host significant baseball games.[3]

Eventually, barnstorming baseball caught the attention of Major League Baseball, and the team owners and executives expressed concern about the exhibition games.

An editorial in the *Chicago Tribune* at the time wrote:

> *"President (Barney) Dreyfuss of the world's champions asked his men to give up the 'barnstorming' trip which a squad of them was planning after the (World Series). He was liable to wake up some morning and read about $70,000 worth of players being beaten by some $7 team. Of course it would be the "Pittsburg world's champions" who were trimmed, even if (Honus) Wagner, (George) Gibson, (Fred) Clarke, (Tommy) Leach, and a few other real world's champions were absent."[9]*

As a result of this extra concern and attention regarding team reputation and player safety, prior to the 1910 season, all new player contracts included the following clause: *"The party of the second part (the player) will not be permitted at any time, either during the playing season or before the commencement or after the close thereof, to participate in any exhibition baseball games, indoor baseball, basketball, or football, except that the consent of the party of the first part (the club) has first been secured in writing."[9]*

This new rule was further expanded upon in February 1921, when Section 8B of Article 4 of the Major League code stated: *"Both teams that contest in the World's Series are required to disband immediately after its close and the members thereof are forbidden to participate as individuals or as a team in exhibition games during the year in which that world's championship was decided."[9]*

The new rule greatly affected barnstormers that year, especially New York Yankees teammates Babe Ruth, Bob Meusel, and Bill Piercy. The three Yankees teammates were all coming off an American League pennant in 1921, and as a result of barnstorming, they were all fined their World Series shares and suspended until May 20 of the 1922 season by Baseball Commissioner Kenesaw

Landis for participating in exhibition games following the 1921 Fall Classic.[9]

After a barnstorming baseball game that took place in Elmira, N.Y. on Oct. 17, 1921, Babe Ruth said:

> *"I am not in any fight to see who is the greatest man in baseball. Meusel, Piercy and I think we are doing something in the interest of baseball. I do not see why we are singled out when other big players, members of second and third place clubs in the World's Series money, are permitted to play post-season games. I am out to earn an honest dollar, and at the same time give baseball fans an opportunity to see the big players in action."* [9]

The barnstorming rule by which Ruth, Meusel, and Piercy were all suspended was removed by July 1922, and shortly after this removal, new rule addendums were added. These included clauses such as: 1) players needed to obtain consent of the club president and the permission of the commissioner to participate in a barnstorming tour, 2) players were not allowed to participate in any exhibition games past October 31, and lastly, 3) no more than three players from any one club were allowed to play on a single team in an exhibition game. [9]

However, as you read earlier from Victor Hugo's diary, *"Nothing, not all the armies of the world, can stop an idea whose time has come."*[1]

The new rule changes led to popular barnstorming tours in the mid-1920s with Babe Ruth and Yankees teammate Lou Gehrig.[9]

Leigh Montville, a Babe Ruth biographer, wrote in his book <u>The Big Bam,</u> *"If you were a pretty good baseball player in the twenties... the chances were pretty good that you played against Babe Ruth at least once in your life."*[13]

During the next 20 years, baseball had what could be considered the Golden Age of barnstorming, as touring teams led by such future Hall of Famers, such as Dizzy Dean, Bob Feller, Satchel Paige, and Jackie Robinson, were all highlights of the tours.[9]

By the 1950s, however, spectators were not attending barnstorming baseball games as often as they had been in previous years. Much of the decline in interest and attendance was a result of the advancements of radio and television coverage of Major League Baseball games.[9]

These changes also affected Parkhurst Field, and in 1955, the Parkhurst family graciously allowed the newly-formed Gloversville Little League to begin playing their baseball games at Parkhurst Field. [3]

Today, Parkhurst Field continues to host Gloversville Little League games every spring and summer, and recently, in 2014, The Parkhurst Field Foundation was formed to help chronicle the ballpark's rich history, as well as revitalize and preserve the park's infrastructure to ensure sustainability.[3]

One of the ways The Parkhurst Field Foundation accomplishes these goals is through hosting baseball tournaments that give young athletes from all over the nation the opportunity to play baseball at the former "A., J. & G Park/now Parkhurst Field" ballpark.

In the years that followed the successful 1907 baseball season, A., J. & G Park, and its spectators, would eventually see a collection of more than 70 future and former Major League Baseball players who played for either the JAGS or who were part of the visiting teams that came to play against the JAGS or other baseball teams. Among these classics included a game on October 13, 1913 that featured an exhibition match where the Philadelphia Athletics pitching ace, Chief Bender, pitched in Gloversville just two days after the Athletics won the 1913 World Series. [3, 4, 12]

In addition, Parkhurst Field is one of the most historic baseball grounds in America. It is older than Fenway Park and Wrigley Field. Cy Young's playing career pre-dates Fenway Park, yet he played on the grounds of Parkhurst Field when it was known as A., J. & G Park. Other than Wrigley Field, and possibly Rickwood Field in Birmingham, Parkhurst Field is one of the few remaining grounds in existence on which Honus Wagner played. Also, it is believed that Parkhurst Field is the only field left in America where the immortalized "Moonlight" Doc Graham played.[3] These stories and more are why Parkhurst Field can truly be considered to be the rarest diamond in the world.

Today, when kids travel to Parkhurst Field, they have the opportunity to experience playing baseball on the same grounds where former ballplayers, such as Honus Wagner, Cy Young, "Moonlight" Doc Graham, Chief Bender, and many more all once stood and played- on "A., J. & G Park"/ "Parkhurst Field".

If the opportunity to play baseball at Parkhurst Field sounds like an experience that you think local ball players and young athletes in your area would enjoy, I would encourage you to contact the Parkhurst Field Foundation to inquire about playing in a tournament. You can contact them by going here: parkhurstfield.org/contact-us

The Parkhurst Field Foundation was also formed in part to help promote and preserve Parkhurst Field in Gloversville, N.Y.- recognized as the "Original Field of Dreams" and as the oldest baseball grounds used by any Little League in America.[3]

Currently, one of the efforts to promote and preserve Parkhurst Field includes plans to rebuild the park to its original glory. These plans include the creation of 5 regulation lighted fields capable of hosting Little League teams from around the country, a premier field that features a smaller scale grandstand (750 seating) similar to the original 1,500 grandstand at A., J. & G Park, batting cages, a new concession stand, and a museum.[3]

The New York State Economic Development Council recently endorsed this $2.3 million project, when the Parkhurst Field Foundation was awarded a grant for $500,000.[3]

If you're wondering who I am or about my involvement in the Parkhurst Field Foundation, my name is Christopher Hallenbeck. In August of 2017, I was asked to speak at a Radio-A-Thon fundraiser in support of Parkhurst Field. Since then, I have continued my support and have been interested in helping promote the opportunities that Parkhurst Field offers to youth, families, and communities, as well as helping support the progress of the foundation's fundraising efforts.

For those reasons, I would like to extend an invitation to you to contact Parkhurst Field if you know of a team that you think would be interested in playing at Parkhurst Field. Also, if you're inclined to support the plans to help rebuild Parkhurst Field to its original glory, there is an opportunity to help contribute financially to The Parkhurst Field Foundation by visiting parkhurstfield.org/product/donate/

In closing, Leigh Montville, a Babe Ruth biographer, once wrote the following about the Babe, "...*His best records weren't recorded in books; they were kept in individual memories of an astounding sight witnessed on a warm afternoon, the memories transferred by word of mouth.*" [13]

To me, this perfectly describes what it must have been like to catch Babe Ruth on one of his classic 1920s barnstorming tours, it describes what the future of Parkhurst Field offers for young athletes, and finally it describes exactly what Mike Hauser has presented for all of us in the baseball short stories inside Hometown Sports Heroes, Vol. 1... all of these experiences providing "*individual memories of an astounding sight witnessed on a warm afternoon, the memories transferred by word of mouth.*" [13]

I hope you enjoy reading Mike Hauser's Hometown Sports Heroes as much as I did, and afterwards, I hope you'll consider supporting Parkhurst Field to help bring kids these astounding sights and create memories for them that they will all surely be transferring by word of mouth for the rest of their lives.

Hometown Sports Heroes Vol. 1

16 Classic Baseball Tales

By: Mike Hauser

Russell Holmes – Gloversville's Fenway Park Connection

"He was the Bullpen Catcher in the summer of '15, when long ago the Red Sox won it all! You won't find him in the record books, he never took a swing, but he knew all there was to know about Babe Ruth's curve ball" are the first two lines from a song called "Free Once More" off the CD "Smokey Joe Wood Throw Back".

The song was written and recorded by Gloversville native Mark Holmes in 2004 about his Grandfather Russell Holmes baseball career.

Russell E. Holmes (nicknamed "Bud") was a journeyman professional baseball player who was born in 1891 in Catskill, NY and grew up in Gloversville, NY as part of the R.E. Holmes Lumber family that owned and operated a lumber business in Bleecker and Gloversville. Holmes learned the family lumber business and played football, basketball and baseball for Gloversville High School. He was the captain and manager of the Gloversville Nine baseball team graduating in 1910.

After high school, Holmes immediately started playing for the Danforth's semi-pro team that played its games at A. J. & G Park/Parkhurst Field in Gloversville. He was with them for the 1910, 1911 and start of the 1912 season and helped them win the Central New York Championship in 1910. Holmes tried out for Connie Mack's Philadelphia Athletics in the spring of 1912. After a few days working out with the team, they were in Newark NJ for an exhibition game and Holmes was put in to play third base as a substitute for future baseball hall of famer Frank "Home Run" Baker.

Six months prior, Holmes had watched Baker at the Polo Grounds in New York account for all 3 runs scored against Christy Matthewson to win Game #3 of the 1911 World Series for the Athletics. Holmes didn't catch on with the Athletics and they sent him to the Spartanburg club in the Carolina Association. While the records aren't as to his playing time that season, he would spend the 1913 and 1914 seasons with Newburgh in the New York-New Jersey League.

He lit up minor league pitching both seasons with a .357 batting average in 1913 and a .336 batting average in 1914. He began the 1915 season with Lewiston (Maine) in the New England League. On opening day, Holmes went 4-4 with two home runs and two singles. A scout for the Boston Red Sox's was in the stands that day to watch a player on the other team and wired back to Boston suggesting they get Holmes before another big league club did. Although the Red Sox already had two catchers, they signed him and delegated him to the bullpen to warm up their pitchers, with the intention that he would be available if any injuries took place to their regular catchers. The staff of pitchers he warmed up and got to know included the legendary Babe Ruth (Ruth actually began his career as a pitcher and compiled 94 Wins before becoming a position player), Ernie Shore and Smokey Joe Wood. Also on the team that season were future hall of famers Herb Pennock, Harry Hooper and Tris Speaker.

According to Holmes, Speaker and his wife Mary would take him for Sunday afternoon drives in their Chalmer 30 Torpedo Roadster around the outskirts of Boston. In 1915, owning a car was a real luxury and not many people (even major leaguers) owned them. Speaker received the vehicle for winning the 1912 Chalmers Award, which was given to the most valuable player in the both the American League & National League from 1911 through 1914. While he never actually got into a game, Holmes did have a front row seat to most of the 1915 season and for the World Series that year in which they defeated the Philadelphia Phillies. It was that same series that Woodrow Wilson became the first US President to attend a World Series Game, and at the urging of Babe Ruth and his other teammates, the Red Sox included Holmes in the sharing of the teams World Series earnings.

In January of 1916 the Red Sox sent Holmes a contract offering him $1,200 for the season. When he refused to sign and asked for an additional $100, they sent him to Buffalo in the International League. He split the 1916 season between Buffalo and Norfolk in the Virginia League. There, he played with and was roommates with future hall of famer Stanley "Bucky" Harris. He and Harris played together again during the 1917 season when their NY State League Teams merged.

During their playing time together they developed a life-long friendship. In fact, Holmes would give his only son Jack the middle name of "Stanley" in honor his former teammate. Holmes also attended Harris' Hall of Fame induction in Cooperstown in 1975. In April 1917, the United States entered World War I.

Shortly thereafter, Holmes left baseball to join his brother Arthur in enlisting in the war effort. They were sent to France as part of the U.S. Army Corps of Engineers 5th Battalion 20th Engineer Regiment (forestry). Both drew from their experience as Adirondack lumberjacks having grown up working for their father's lumber company, to help the Corp produce over 200 million feet of lumber to aid in building bridges, roads, tent poles/stakes and fighting trenches. Russell was honorably discharged as a Sergeant in 1919, returned to Fulton County and married Mildred Hornett. That season he played for both the local Sacandaga's semi-pro team and another in Windsor VT honing his skills to get back into professional baseball. He spent three more seasons in professional baseball with stops at Richmond in the Virginia League (1920), Morristown in the Appalachian League (1921) and with Danville in the Piedmont League in Virginia (1922).

His first child was born in 1922 and at the end of the season he decided to return to Gloversville where he worked as a silk weaver and tanner and raised his family of three children; Dorothy, John (Jack) & Marjorie at 96 6th Avenue. Although his professional career was over, his life in baseball was far from over.

He would continue to play for, coach and umpire local semi-pro teams into the 1940's. In 1986 when the Boston Red Sox reached the World Series, it was believed that he was the last surviving member of their championship teams of the pre-1920's. When Holmes turned 100 years old in 1991, he received a letter from the Boston Red Sox (signed by the entire team) honoring him with the distinction of being the oldest living former member of their organization.

Holmes was a lifelong member of the Foothills United Methodist Church, and at the age 97 moved to the Wells Nursing Home in Johnstown. He died on July 12, 1993 at the age of 102. While he never fulfilled his dream of getting a Major League at bat, he played with and against many of the games early legends.

Holmes was inducted into the Fulton County Baseball & Sports Hall of Fame on July 10, 2016 at Parkhurst Field in Gloversville, the site where he caught in hundreds of games as a high schooler, semi-professional and post professional career exhibition player. The induction took place between innings of a vintage baseball game between the Whatley Pioneers of Western Massachusetts and the A., J. & G. Team of Fulton County.

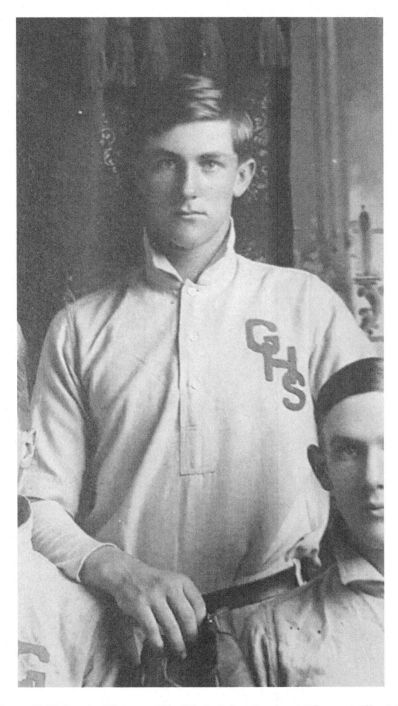

Russell Holmes, Gloversville High School, 1909, Gloversville, NY

Russell Holmes at Fenway Park in Boston, Massachusetts

Danforth's Baseball Team – 1910.
(Russell Holmes is back row, all the way to right, next to door)

Russell Holmes featured on the cover of his grandson Mark
Holmes, CD, "Throwback"

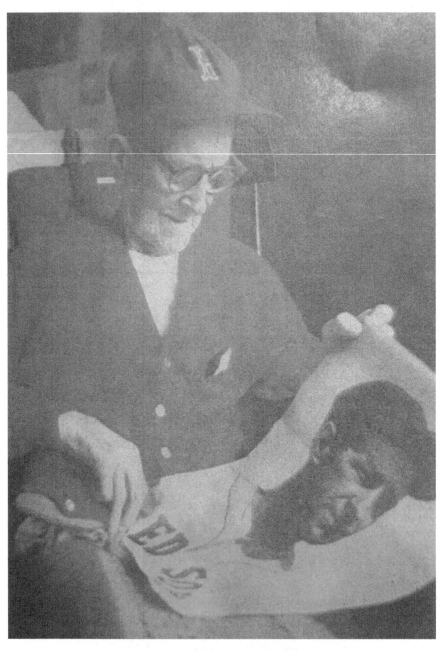

Russell Holmes on his 100th Birthday
holding a photo of Bucky Harris.

Grimshaw brings the big leagues, Cy Young to Gloversville

As I drive by the former Beech Nut Plant in Canajoharie, it reminds me of a former major league baseball player who worked there and also led their company baseball team as a player & manager in his later years. His name was Myron Frederick Grimshaw and he was born in St. Johnsville NY in 1875 and grew up in Canajoharie NY. Known as "Kitsie" in his hometown,

Grimshaw went on to play professional baseball from 1898 until 1911. He spent much of his youth playing on local town teams and began his professional career at the age of 23 playing for the London Cockneys in the Canadian League in 1898.

The following season he split time between the Guelph Maple Leafs of the same league, as well as the Ilion team of the New York State League. After spending the 1900 season back in Canada with the Chatham Reds, he spent the next four seasons with the Buffalo Bison's of the Eastern League. He batted .317 (1901), .297 (1902), .325 (1903) and .355 (1904) and led the Eastern League in runs scored (98) and hits (177).

Writer Tim Murnane from the Boston Globe watched him play late in the 1904 season and wrote *"they tell me here, that Grimshaw is one of the finest batsmen in the business and a clever first baseman."* He also mentioned how Grimshaw's four hits the day before had helped the Bison's win a doubleheader and believed that he would strengthen Jimmy Collin's Boston American's Club (Red Sox) which was in the process of competing for its second straight American League Pennant. They won the very first modern-day World Series over the Pittsburgh Pirates the year before.

Based on this, Boston purchased Grimshaw's contract in early September 1904, expecting he would immediately join the team in Boston for the remainder of the season. But the Bison's were also in contention for the Eastern League Pennant, so Grimshaw stayed in Buffalo for the remainder of the season.

In 1905, he joined the Boston Americans for spring training and impressed their star third baseman and future hall of famer Jimmy Collins as he battled for the first base job against incumbent George "Candy" LaChance. Collins was quoted as saying *"Big George is hitting weaker than ever in his life, while Grimshaw looms up big as a house."* It is believed that this statement would in turn give Grimshaw the nickname of "Moose" as he was known thereafter. He made the big league club that spring and joined the team in Boston where they played their games at the Huntington Avenue Fairgrounds (Fenway Park would not be built until 1912). He played 85 games at first base despite battling a severe case of Malaria that season. According to the American League physician Dr. Erb, he had never seen a worse case of Malaria than Grimshaw's. Despite his illness, he batted .239 that season and tied for the team lead in home runs with 4. Collins, who had been complimentary of Grimshaw in spring training was not sympathetic towards Grimshaw's season. He stated that *"Grimshaw was too timid this year and for that reason he didn't do as well as he could."*

As soon as the season ended, Boston owner John I. Taylor attempted to trade Grimshaw to Minneapolis for first baseman Jerry Freeman. However, a few other teams claimed him, so he did not clear waivers. It was eventually ruled by American League President Ban Johnson that the trade couldn't take place, which kept him with the Boston Club. Grimshaw was hurt by the trade attempt, but after a winter of fishing and hunting in the Adirondacks during the offseason, he came back healthy and ready to claim the first base job with Boston as his. He reported to spring training in Macon GA in 1906 in great shape and regained the first baseman's job.

However, injuries during the season (hurt kneecap in April and broken wrist in July) limited him to just 110 games. Despite the injuries and missing 50 games, he still led the team with a batting average of .290 and had 48 RBI's (team leader had only 51). In 1907 he came back to Boston and split time between first base and the outfield.

On July 5, 1907 while on route from Boston to Detroit to play the Tigers, Grimshaw and the entire Boston team stopped in Gloversville to play an exhibition game. The game took place at A., J. & G Park (now Parkhurst Field) against the A., J. & G. team that played there in the New York State League. Because of the proximity to Grimshaw's hometown, the team made the stop to play the game knowing that lots of Grimshaw's family & friends from the

Mohawk Valley would make the trip to see the game. As expected, the crowds were large and the visiting Boston team beat the locals by a score of 8-3. Although normally a first baseman and outfielder, Grimshaw played short stop that day. One newspaper stated *"the battery of Reardon and Cooney for the locals was a feature, while in fielding Grimshaw at short for the visitors was worth the price of admission alone"*.

Another thrill for Fulton & Montgomery County Fans was that future Hall of Famer Cy Young was part of the game as the Boston Americans player/manager. While he didn't play in that game, he was certainly a big-league star, having already compiled over 450 of the 511 pitching wins he would earn during his career.

The 1907 season was his last year in the Major Leagues and he returned to Canada to play for the Toronto Maple Leafs in the Eastern League for the next three seasons. He was limited to just 18 games in 1908 after having his collar bone broken by a pitched ball. In 1909 he came bounced back to lead the entire Eastern League with a .309 batting average. It was during this same year that he was featured on a baseball card in the famous T-206 baseball card set. This set contained 524 different players, 76 of which were future inductees into the Baseball Hall of Fame, including the highly regarded Honus Wagner card that sold for over $2,800,000 in 2011. Twelve variations of Grimshaw's card in this set are known to exist.

Grimshaw frustrated the Toronto club in 1909 and 1910 by showing up at the very last minute for spring training without sending word that he was returning to the team. It was believed that he was deep in the Adirondacks both years guiding hunters and could not be bothered. He batted .287 in 1910 after having his season ended in July when he was hit in the ear with a pitch that knocked him unconscious. It crushed his ear drum and left him hemorrhaging from his ear for quite some time. It was thought that his career was over, but he recuperated and was transferred to Louisville for the 1911 season where he once again came back from serious injury and batted .363 . In 1912 he was transferred to Indianapolis in the American Association, but refused to report and sat out the 1912 & 1913 seasons. Early in 1914 the Louisville club finally released him and his professional career was over.

In April of 1914 he began working for the Beech Nut Corporation in Canajoharie as a night watchman. That same spring he joined the semi-pro Danforth's Team that played in the Sunset League at A., J. & G. Park in Gloversville. In 1915 he was named the Danforth's player/manager. By mid-season in 1915 the Danforth's team disbanded due to lack of patronage and he was immediately signed by the Amsterdam Empires semi-pro team for the remainder of the season. In 1919 he joined the Beech Nut semi-pro team as their player/manager and now combined work with pleasure. He would spend the next several seasons with the Beech Nuts and other local semi-pro teams in the Mohawk Valley.

The last documented game he played in was an old timers game in July 1934 (at age 58) alongside of former New York Giant star George Burns. He would also be called upon regularly to speak to church groups and men's groups to talk about his baseball career, while continuing to work at Beech Nut. After working as night watchman and a laborer at Beech Nut for many years, Grimshaw eventually became superintendent of shipping. On the morning of December 11, 1936 he suffered a heart attack at work and died later that day at his home at the age of 61.

In July of 1939, his widow Mabel was invited to Cooperstown by the Centennial Committee celebrating baseball's 100th anniversary to be a special guest at the "Connie Mack Day" game at Doubleday Field between the Philadelphia Athletics and the Penn Athletic Club. On that trip she viewed articles of her husband's baseball gear that she had donated to the committee to be included in the newly created permanent exhibit at the National Baseball Hall of Fame that had opened just a few weeks prior.

Grimshaw was inducted into the Fulton County Baseball & Sports Hall of Fame on July 10, 2016 at Parkhurst Field in Gloversville, the site where he played & managed dozens of semi-professional games during his post professional career. The inductions took place between innings of a Vintage Baseball Game that took place between the Whatley Pioneers of Western Massachusetts and the A., J. & G. Team of Fulton County.

Moose Grimshaw in his Buffalo Bison uniform.

Young
Stahl
Hayden
Ferris
Grimshaw
Parent

A GROUP OF BOSTON AMERICANS.

Boston Americans Team Collage.

Grimshaw playing, batting, and field in Chicago with the Red Sox.

Moose Grimshaw Beech Nut Team Picture from newspaper.

Grimshaw as an old man in a Boston uniform sitting in the grass.

Schumacher - Upstate New York's Prince of Baseball

Harold Henry Schumacher was born in Hinckley NY in 1910 and grew up in Dolgeville NY, where he was a three sport star at Dolgeville High School excelling in Football, Basketball and Baseball. In 1924 at the age of 14 (and in the 8th grade) he became the starting pitcher and lead-off hitter on the varsity baseball team.

After four very successful seasons as a varsity starter and considered one of the best high school pitchers in Upstate NY, he was ineligible to play for the high school team during his senior year (1928) because he had already used up his four years of eligibility. Instead, the 17 year-old started pitching for the Spofford Hose Company town team in the Eastern New York Press League at Hilltop Park in Dolgeville.

In the first few weeks of the season pitching against grown men, he struck out 20 & 22 in a game and started drawing large crowds each time he pitched. By mid-June of that spring (and still in high school) he was signed to play semi-pro baseball for the Little Falls Team in the Utica Daily Press League. Due to professional eligibility rules, he would have to wait until he officially graduated from high school and then started his first semi-professional game against the Gloversville Nine Team on July 1, 1928.

After a successful season in which he played for both the Dolgeville and Little Falls teams, he enrolled in college at St. Lawrence University in Canton NY where he continued to play football, basketball and baseball. After his first year at St. Lawrence he was back with the Spofford Hose Team during the summer of 1929. His starts would attract record crowds that usually Included Major League Scouts. After a hot stretch in the spring of 1930 during his sophomore year with St. Lawrence in which he struck out 54 over 3 games, he was offered a contract by the New York Yankees. Hal turned down the offer, telling the Yankees that would not entertain professional offers until he finished his college education.

During the summer of 1930 he would again rejoin his hometown Spofford Hose Team to keep in shape. Later that summer, he was approached by New York Giants Scout Art Devlin offering a chance for him to play for the Giants. While the 19 year-old had said no to the New York Yankees offer just a few months prior, being approached by a team willing to entertain his wanting to continue college intrigued him. That fall (1930) Schumacher was invited to New York City to meet with Giants manager John J. McGraw. Although Schumacher did not sign a formal contract that day, it was established by McGraw that the Giants were interested in him and encouraged him to return to college to continue to pursue his college degree. He finished out his fall semester and then officially signed a contract with the Giants in January of 1931 at the age of 20, with the caveat that he would be allowed to complete his college education. He and was then granted a temporary leave by St. Lawrence so he could join the Giants in San Antonio TX for spring training. However, St. Lawrence stipulated that he would need to keep up his course work in the off-season and stay on track to graduate on time.

In spring training he would be put under the tutelage of future Hall of Fame Pitcher Charles "Chief" Bender and George J. Burns who was also from the Mohawk Valley area and was a player that Hal admired as a young boy. Both former players were signed that year as coaches to work with young players. Schumacher would make the Giants big league team out of spring training and with the exception of a five-week stint in the minors late that season, would never spend another day in the minors in a career that would last from 1931 to 1946. As a rookie in 1931, Hal had 2 starts, with 1 win, 1 loss and 1 save. After the season ended in September Hal was back at the St. Lawrence campus for the fall & winter semesters.

The 1932 season would see him get 13 starts with the Giants, pitch 2 complete games and finish with a record of 5 wins and 6 losses. Once again after the season was over he was enrolled back at classes at St. Lawrence for the fall and winter semesters. By doubling up on his course loads, he completed the course requirements to graduate before he reported to spring training in February of 1933.

The 1933 season would be the breakout season that would define Schumacher as one of the best pitchers in baseball and cement his place in baseball lore on several levels. That season, he pitched 21 complete games, won 19 and had a 2.16 ERA. A career year for most professionals, but not even the most unique things about his season. St. Lawrence University held their graduation ceremonies on June 12th, which was right in the middle of the Major League Baseball season. Not only was Schumacher allowed to travel to Canton NY to attend to ceremony to receive his diploma, but the entire New York Giants team made the trip with him.

This marked the first time in history that an active MLB player received a college degree, as well as the first time that a MLB team would honor a teammate by attending their graduation ceremony. Another first was that the Giants suited up to play a game against the St. Lawrence University baseball team immediately following the ceremony. It was estimated that nearly 10,000 spectators converged on Canton NY, which normally had a population of only 2,000 to view the ceremonies and game. Hal pitched the first two innings of the game in which the Giants beat his former team by a score of 12-4.

A few weeks later on July 6, 1933 Major League Baseball held its very first All-Star Game that pitted the best of the National League against the best of the American League. Future Hall of Fame Manager John McGraw was named to manage the National League team and chose Schumacher to represent the Giants on his squad.

Many years later Schumacher told me that he was not upset at the time that he had not gotten into the game to pitch because it was only an exhibition and that he was just happy to be there to watch all the legends he had idolized growing up. Looking back 55 years later he said that knowing what a big deal the game had become, he wished he had played. To cap off this incredible season, the New York Giants won the National League Pennant and went on to beat the Washington Senators 4 games to 1 in the World Series. Hal had two starts in the series and took one of those starts to a complete game win in Game 2. It was this season that Hal would earn the nickname of "Prince Hal" as a complement his teammate's "King Carl" Hubbell, as they made up the most feared pitching duo in the Major Leagues.

Hal would get his chance to pitch in an All-Star Game when he was voted in to play in the 1935 contest. This time he pitched four complete innings, gave up 1 run and struck out future Hall of Famers Jimmie Foxx, Joe Cronin and Al Simmons. In 1936 the Giants got back to the World Series and faced the New York Yankees and a line-up that featured eight future Hall of Famers. Hal and the Giants were beaten up quite badly in Game 2 by a score of 18-4. Hal would bounce back with a win in Game 5 with a 10 inning gem that beat the Yankees by a score of 5-4. It was in this game that Hal lived every young boy's dream of that big World Series moment. It came in the 5th inning with bases loaded and no outs. Due up at the plate was Joe DiMaggio, with Lou Gehrig on deck and Bill Dickey behind him. Hal responded by striking out both DiMaggio and Gehrig and getting Dickey to pop up for the third out of the inning.

Hal would meet success for the rest of his career which lasted through 1946. He would miss the 1943-45 seasons due to serving as a Navy Lieutenant in WWII aboard the USS Cape Esperance in the Pacific Fleet. Over his career, he would start 329 games, and compile a record of 158-121. 137 of those outings were complete games and 27 were shut outs, for a 3.36 career ERA. He would pitch in at total of four World Series Games (1933, 1936 & 1937) with a record of 2-2. At the plate, he was known as a very good hitter for a pitcher. He hit 6 home runs 1934 which was the National League record at the time, but would eventually be broken in 1955 by Don Newcombe. In total, he hit 15 home runs in his career which still ranks him at 20th on the all-time career list for pitchers.

Upon retiring from Baseball as a player after the 1946 season, Hal returned home to Dolgeville where he purchased an interest in the McLaughlin-Millard company that was located in his hometown. The company had previously manufactured bowling pins, toboggans and other wood products. They had recently turned their focus to turning out baseball bats made of Northern White Ash from the area and hired Hal to be their vice president and sales manager. Using his contacts in the baseball world, Hal visited Major League training camps and signed players to use their bats.

Getting players to use the product would prove to be a great catalyst to get amateur players in youth leagues to also purchase them. This marked the birth of the Adirondack Bat and by 1957 they were selling over 1,000,000 bats per year. The company was eventually purchased by Rawlings Sporting Goods and still manufactures a large percentage of the bats used by Major League players today. Hal left the bat manufacturing business in 1967 and went to work for Little League International at their Williamsport PA headquarters in the spring of 1968. After helping the organization set up instructional programs for its players, he retired back to

Dolgeville and summered at his family cottage on Canada Lake that they had purchased in the 1950's.

He would Golf several times each week at Nick Stoner Golf Course, as well as other local courses across Fulton County. He also made many appearances in retirement as a speaker at banquets and signing autographs at Baseball Card Shows. According to Peg Johnston at Dick & Pegs Northward Inn, she remembers Hal and his wife Alice dining at her family's restaurant during the summer and that he always obliged fans who asked for his autograph. She stated that he also gave each young autograph seeker a dollar as a thank you for remembering and acknowledging him. Hal passed away on April 21, 1993 at Imogene Bassett Hospital in Cooperstown at the age of 82. He is the only former Major Leaguer to pass away in Cooperstown.

Schumacher was inducted into the Fulton County Baseball & Sports Hall of Fame on July 10, 2016 at Parkhurst Field in Gloversville. The inductions took place between innings of a vintage baseball game taking place between the Whatley Pioneers of Western Massachusetts and the A., J. & G. Team of Fulton County.

Hal Schumacher in his New York Giants hat.

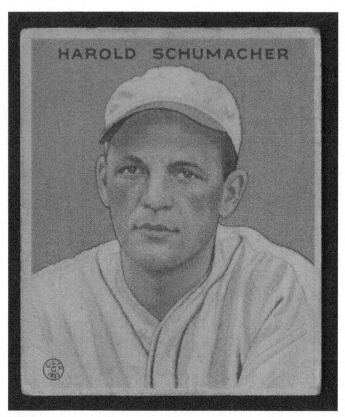

A collection of Hal Schumacher autographed photos.

Unsigned photos of Hal Schumacher at the Dolgeville Bat Plant.

Chickens, Tigers & Pirates...Mayfield Baseball of course

Over the last few years, much has been documented about Gloversville's Historic baseball diamonds that once featured big time ball games and brought professional and world class exhibition teams to our area. A., J. & G Park/Parkhurst Field and Glovers Park are the fields that come to mind, and the JAGS & Glovers are the teams we associate with them.

A few miles to the north, the village of Mayfield and the hamlet of Riceville can also stake early claims to organized baseball here in Fulton County. A few years ago, a co-worker named Mary Weber gave me a Mayfield Old Home Day Baseball Souvenir program that belonged to her mother (Jeff) Alice Zimmerman Czupryk.

The program advertised a game that was played on August 7, 1920 between the Mayfield Tigers vs. Sacandagas. On the back of the program were roster listings for Mayfield teams called "The Chickens" from 1885 through 1905. A sampling of some of the player's names include; Frank Goodemote, Craz Danforth, Marv Fonda, George Hathaway, Louie Jerome, Rube Wilson, Cornie Satterlee, Zeiby Bixby, Fat Warner, Ralph Dingman, Tuddle Wilkins, Fritz Warner, Fred Bennett, and Tommie Donlon.

These "Chicken" teams were town teams made up exclusively of Mayfield residents who played their games against other rural area town teams. They initially received that name because most of the players were less than twenty years of age (spring chickens). While young, they were not afraid to take on any challenges and were quite successful. The exact location of their first games is not known for sure. There is mention of them playing at the old Riceville & Sam Brown plots. These early teams grew up with the game and its early rules making it a much different game than today. Batters calling their desired pitch zone, restricted pitching motions and fielders using gloves more resembling "batting gloves" of present day resulted in those youngsters nursing red unprotected hands after each game. To get a glimpse of what those games were like one can attend the annual Vintage Baseball Game that takes place each summer at Parkhurst Field using the rules of Major League Baseball from 1886.

Around the beginning of the 1900's, there is mention of teams using a ball field that was laid out in the "new section" of the Mayfield Union Rural Cemetery. The entire cemetery was initially laid out behind the former Low Dutch Reformed Church that was organized by the Reverend Conradt Ten Eyck in 1793 on Main Street in the village and is now designated by a historical road marker. The field was used until approximately 1918, as the first headstone that appears on the "new section of the cemetery" where the baseball field was is dated 1919.

In the spring of 1920, the community formally organized a new team called the Mayfield Tigers. A group of officers were selected and Walker (Squaker) LaRowe was named the manager. The team included; Prof. McCausland, Kee Kasagi, Squaker La Rowe, Harv Richardson, Ray Parramore, Rufe Gifford, Uty Eutemark and Dizzy De Graff. They also signed Gloversville baseball legend Stewart "Pickles" O'Brien to play for them.

They played their games at a new field that was laid out on a lot next to the cemetery where Maple Avenue & Woodside Avenue meet (houses now cover the area). This piece of land was sandy and not optimal to be used as a serious baseball field. As the season progressed, improvements were made and fans began to attend to support the team. The season ran from the end of May until early September and consisted of 31 games against other area "town teams" in which the Tigers went 21-10.

When the 1921 season started, subscriptions (donations) were received from local fans to help front expense money to start the season. With these funds, plans were made for better exhibitions to please the fans and more "non-Mayfield players" were signed to play. This new formula of using the most talented players from the area proved so successful (better play and drew a larger fan base from both Mayfield & Gloversville) that the team moved to a new field that was built in the hamlet of Riceville halfway through the season.

Bearing in mind that this was before the new/straighter Route 30A was built in the 1960's, the field set off the area that is now between Sundaes Ice Cream Stand (Mr. Softees) on the corner of 2nd Avenue/old Route 30A (Riceville Road) and the Rice Homestead. One newspaper account stated that *"the new Riceville Baseball Diamond is one of the finest in this section of the state because of its dry, firm soil"*.

Dressing rooms and covered bleachers were also added and the team started being referred to as the "Mayfield Bannertown Tigers". This fine ball park and larger fan base enabled the team to start bringing in top area teams such as the Danforth's of Gloversville, the Twin Cities Team of Fonda, and the Johnstown Buckskins. The Tigers won 34 and lost only 9 games that season.

In 1922, the Tigers started recruiting players from the Troy & Albany areas and also secured the services of Gloversville native's Frank Gill & Russell "Bud" Holmes. Gill was one of the top collegiate players in the country when he played for Princeton University, and Holmes had just finished an eleven year professional career that included being part of the 1915 World Champion Boston Red Sox.

The addition of Holmes, Gill and other top players enabled the Tigers to compete against top teams from across the Northeast such as D&H Generals of Troy, the Green Island Knights of Columbus, the Dunns of Albany, Utica Kaysees, the Schenectady Knights of Columbus, the Amsterdam Knights of Columbus , and teams from North Adams MA and Glens Falls. Attendance averaged 300-500 per game, and special exhibition contests brought in as many as 1,200 spectators. Such exhibition games included contests against world class Negro League Teams.

In September of the 1922 season, the Champion Colored baseball team called the Brooklyn Royal Giants played in an exhibition game at the Riceville Diamond. This team was famed throughout the country and known to be a Major League Team of color.

An added bonus for area fans was that local Major Leaguer and 1921 World Series Champion George J. Burns participated in the game as one of the umpires. Burns, a Gloversville resident in the off season, was currently a star outfielder for the Cincinnati Reds. This marked the first time in many years that he had appeared on an area field. While he did not play in the game (the MLB season was still underway and it was an off day), he did practice with the teams before the game, which was a big thrill for local fans.

The local Tigers squad won a tightly played game by the score of 5-4 thanks to "impossible catches" and a clutch bottom of the ninth inning rally complete with a walk off single by Tigers second baseman Scovic.

In May of 1923, the Cuban Stars of Havana Club (Cuban Giants) invaded the Riceville Diamond as the highest paid colored team and one of the best attractions procurable. The team was led by legendary Cuban/Negro League manager Alex Pompez (inducted into the Cooperstown HOF in 2006) and featured center fielder Alejandro Ohms who was considered the *"Babe Ruth of colored baseball teams"* at that time. The Cuban team won a pitching duel over the Pirates by the slim margin of 1-0.

By 1925, other local communities saw the success of semi-pro ball in Mayfield and resurrected teams in their own towns. Gloversville, Johnstown and Broadalbin created new teams, which reduced the patronage of games at the Riceville Diamond. The Tigers disbanded, but the field was taken over by the Mayfield Athletic Association "Inter-Shop Baseball League". This league was made up local glove shops that operated in Mayfield and concluded each season with a "Little World Series".

In the late 1920's a new semi-pro team called the Mayfield Pirates resumed high level baseball at the Riceville Diamond. They continued to bring in the top semi-pro teams from the northeast, as well as highly sought after traveling exhibition teams. On May 27, 1936, the original Cuban Stars of Havana Club returned to play in Mayfield. This time, the Mayfield team got the best of them with a 7-6 victory. Many local Negro teams such as the Schenectady Black Sox and the Mohawk Colored Giants ventured to Mayfield to take on the Pirates throughout the 1930's and 1940's.

In 1949, the first Heisman Trophy Winner Larry Kelley (Yale University 1936) played first base for the Pirates for the entire season. Why this historic football player was in the area will be the subject of a future story.

Records show the Pirates playing at the Riceville Diamond up until 1957. But as the television became prevalent in most homes, people began to stay home to watch Major Leaguers from the comfort of their own couches, rather than physically attend games at local parks to watch semi-professional players play.

While local high school and youth leagues periodically used the diamond in the late 1950's and early 1960's, once the new Route 30A Arterial came through Mayfield in 1966, the original field was disrupted and baseball eventually came to an end at the site.

Today, the site is occupied by the RMF Motor Sports Garage. Home plate is estimated to be where the back corner of the garage nearest Sundaes Ice Cream stand is and the entire building occupies what would have been most of the infield. Third base is in the culvert next to the Arterial and the left field portion of the field is now paved highway. The Center Field and Right Field areas are the still open expanses of the current property.

A special "History of Mayfield Baseball Exhibit" is on display at the Riceville Homestead in Mayfield. The exhibit honored Mayfield's Baseball history dating back to 1884 and up through modern day Mayfield professional players Babe Baldwin and Randy Marshall. The homestead is located at 328 Riceville Road in Mayfield, NY and sits adjacent to the Riceville baseball diamond site.

BACK ROW LEFT TO RIGHTJim Hickey, Roy Wilkins,Harry Timmerman ?
Emery Tyler,Willard DeGraff (Dissey Day)
MIDDLE ROW Joe Bennett, Louie Jerome, Ralph Dingman, Frank (Bob)
Warner, Frank (Fat) Warner
FRONT ROW Ernest Wilkins, Friday Chapman, Roy Millis
                    1894 Ball Team

1894 Mayfield Tigers Baseball Team.

1920
Tigers

Season 1920

THE MAYFIELD TIGERS

Top--Left to Right---Prof. McCausland, Kee Kasagi, Squaker La Rowe, Harv Richardson, Ray Parramore, Pickles O'Brien.

Center--Left to Righ--Rufe Gifford, Uty Eutemark, Dizzy De Graff, Umpire, Bunnie Behlen, Treas., Rat Martling, Johnnie Gifford.

Lower--Nelson Wilkins, Assistant Treasurer.

Willis Warner, Score Keeper, Brick Brower, Sub.

FRONT JAY VAN BUREN - HOWARD MONTAN
1st row FOGAR WARNER - B BECKER - OLIVER VAN BUREN -
HARRY DAVISON - RALPH MONTANYE - HARVEY RICHARDSON -
GORDON BEECH
REAR - WILLYS WARNER - KENNETH DAVISON -
    CLARENCE BECKER - FRANK HILLSON, MGR.

                                                1928

B.E.B.

1928 Mayfield Tigers Baseball Team.

Mayfield Tigers Baseball team. (date of picture unknown)

Mayfield Tigers Baseball game advertisement.

Mayfield Tigers Baseball team.

Jack McKeon...Back to his Gloversville Roots

On July 17, 2016 baseball legend Jack McKeon was in Troy, NY to scout the Florida Marlins A level Batavia Muckdogs as they took on the Houston Astro's A level Tri-City Valley Cats at Joseph L. Bruno Stadium. McKeon is the only manager to win 1,000 games in the Minor Leagues (1398) and 1,000 games in the Major Leagues (1051). He also holds the distinction of being the oldest man to win a World Series, when he guided the Florida Marlins over the New York Yankees back in 2003 at the age of 72. He had a playing career of 10 seasons in the Minor Leagues and has been managing at the professional level since 1955, with 16 of those seasons at the Big League Level with Kansas City (Royals), Oakland (A's), San Diego (Padres), Cincinnati (Reds) and Florida (Marlins). Along the way, he also picked up National League Manager of the Year Awards in 1999 & 2003 and had the distinction of managing the National League All-Stars in the 75th All-Star Game in 2004. Today at the age of 85, he is still an active member of the Miami Marlins organization where he works as a special advisor to the Marlins owner Jeffrey Loria.

For McKeon, a trip to Upstate NY would not be complete without a visit to his old stomping grounds of 1950...Gloversville. In the summer of 1950, the then 19-year-old Perth Amboy, NJ native John (Jack) Mckeon was assigned to get behind the plate for the Gloversville Glovers of the Canadian-American League for 72 games. This marked McKeon's second season in professional baseball and part of the roots of a career that is still going strong 67 years later.

Upon arriving in Gloversville, we toured all of the memorable spots from his 1950 season. There was the old Kingsboro Hotel on South Main Street (now the Kingsboro Apartments) where he reported upon arriving in Gloversville and spent his first few nights in town. One block up on North Main Street was the site of the former Pederick's Diner (now The Romano Acro Dance Academy) where he and most of the Glovers ate the majority of their meals and socialized. A few blocks further North at 50 Yale Street we visited the former Gunneson Family home. They were his host family and let him stay with them during the season. The tour then made a stop at the Fulton County Museum where a "Jack McKeon Exhibit" makes up a portion of the "History of Fulton County Baseball Timeline Display". This marked his first visit to the museum and he was amazed to see all of the items he has given to me over the years sitting there on display to be shared with the sports fans of Fulton County. In addition to items depicting him as a Gloversville Glover, there are photos and cards that document his 16 seasons as a Major League Manager as well as an autographed photo of him and the entire Marlins Team being greeted by President George W. Bush at the White House in January 2004 after winning the World Series. Other notable items include the Florida Marlins hat he wore during the 2003 World Series and the game ball from his 900th Major League Win. During the visit, McKeon personally made some additions to the display, including the December 29, 2003 issue of Sports Illustrated that included he and Carmelo Anthony on the cover.

McKeon's next stop in Gloversville was to visit the former Glovers Park site where he once toiled behind the plate catching for the likes of Gloversville Pitching Icons John Coakley and Loren Stewart. The site is now home to the Runnings Store, Hannaford Super Market and House of Pizza Restaurant. As we stood just inside the entrance to the Running's store chatting with store manager Gary Preusser, he pointed out that we were standing right about where second base used to be. McKeon responded with "so this is where I broke my ankle sliding into second base". After reminiscing about the 1950 season, and then signing some autographs and posing for pictures, he made his way up to the entrance to the site in front of The House of Pizza Restaurant (on 5th Avenue) to officially dedicate a Fulton County Sports Historical Road Marker. There we were greeted by owner Gus Avgerakis, who was generous enough to allow us to place the Marker on his property, and the family of former Gloversville Glover Pitcher (and lifelong friend of McKeon) John Coakley. This group helped McKeon with the unveiling of a Road Marker that denotes the history of Glovers Park dating back to the 1800's when it was called Berkshire Fairgrounds / Past Time Park and hosted Horse, Dog and Auto Racing, as well as other sporting events. The next time you are dining there at the House of Pizza (or driving in to shop at Runnings or Hannaford's), you won't be able to miss it.

On the way out of town to catch his evening game in Troy, McKeon's last stop was Parkhurst Field, the site of the final game he ever managed. Back on October 12, 2013, Jack came out of retirement as a manager to guide the A., J. & G.'s against former Major Leaguer Jim Bouton and the Whately Pioneers of Western Massachusetts in a Vintage Baseball Game played using the Rules & Equipment standard in 1886. The game was part of the 2013 Fulton County

Baseball & Sports Hall of Fame Inductions, and McKeon successfully guided the A., J.& G.'s (former Gloversville Little League Alumni) to an 11-7 win over the Pioneers, marking his 2450th and final win as a manager to date (1051 Major League / 1398 Minor League/ 1 Vintage League). It was also on that same day that he helped dedicate another historical road marker that denotes that baseball has been played at A., J. & G. Park / Parkhurst Field since 1906. The Parkhust Field Museum which is located at the park documents the McKeon Vintage Game, as well as the entire history of the park from 1906-present.

As we drove into Troy to end the tour, Jack stated "it is always exciting to go back to places you once played. But to be remembered like I am here (Gloversville) 65 years later is very unique and flattering." To see the imprint that Gloversville has had on McKeon (and vice versa), you can see the "Jack McKeon Exhibit" at the Fulton County Museum. The museum is located at 237 Kingsboro Avenue and open on Saturdays and Sunday (Noon-4pm) through May through October and on Saturdays (9am-Noon) throughout the winter. The historical road markers that McKeon has a part in at A., J. & G. Park / Parkhurst Field (Harrison Street) and Glovers Park (5th Avenue) are on display year-round and the Parkhurst Field Museum (Harrison Street) is open anytime a Gloversville Little League game is taking place (May-August).

Jack McKeon when he played baseball
for The Gloversville Glovers in 1950.

Jack McKeon in his Gloversville Glovers uniform.

2012 Vintage Baseball Game, Parkhurst Field, Gloversville, NY. (left to right) Jack McKeon, Dave Karpinksi, Mark "Pres" Pieraccini, and Andy Fusco

Dedication of "A.,J & G. Park" Historical Roadside Marker.
October 13, 2013 Parkhurst Field, Gloversville, NY.
(left to right) Michael Hauser, Mark Pieraccini,
Michael Karpinksi, Jack McKeon, Dave Karpinski

Jack McKeon adds to the "McKeon Display" at The Fulton County Museum, located at 237 Kingsboro Ave., Gloversville, NY.

Jack McKeon points to his 2012 Fulton County Hall of Fame plaque that hangs on the wall in his home office.

Pittsburgh Pirates once visited Gloversville's Berkshire Park

Recently, Upstate New York's Doubleday Field welcomed in retired professional players to suit up for an exhibition game of baseball called the "Hall of Fame Classic". From 1940 to 2008 the event was called the "Hall of Fame Game" and featured two Major League Teams full of current players. These traditional in-season exhibition games got their start in 1939 as part of the celebration of the newly formed National Baseball Hall of Fame just down the street from Doubleday Field. To help dedicate the newly formed Hall of Fame, two teams of current and former major league players representing the 16 baseball clubs at the time were formed. The teams where captained by Eddie Collins (who was being inducted that year) and Honus Wagner, who was a member of the inaugural induction class in 1936.

Two years prior to this (and just one year after being inducted into the Hall of Fame), Honus Wagner and the Pittsburgh Pirates Major League baseball team came to Gloversville to play an exhibition game against the Gloversville Glovers professional baseball team of the Class C Canadian-American League. The Gloversville Glovers had begun playing at Berkshire Park (aka Pastime Park & Glovers Park) on Elmwood Avenue (now the site of the Runnings Supply Store/Hannaford Grocery Store/House of Pizza Restaurant) the year before, marking the return of professional baseball to Gloversville for the first time since the A., J & G's of the New York State league played at A., J. & G Park (Parkhurst Field) from 1906 to 1908. The date was Monday July 26, 1937, and the Pirates had finished a weekend series at Braves Field in Boston against the Boston Bees (fore runner to the Boston Braves and eventually the Atlanta Braves) and were in route back to Pittsburgh for a game on Wednesday July 27th against the Philadelphia Phillies at Forbes Field.

Upon arriving in Gloversville on the morning of July 26th, the Pirates checked into the Hotel Kingsborough on South Main Street (now the 'Kingsboro' Apartments) at around 10am in order to get a few hours rest before a late afternoon game with the Glovers. Several hundred baseball fans where at the hotel to greet the team and a traffic jam ensued on South Main Street. Two of the greeters in the hotel lobby were former professional baseball player and future Fulton County Baseball & Sports Hall of Fame member Russell (Bud) Holmes and his 11 year-old son Jack. Holmes had played against the Pirates Manager Pie Traynor when they were both Major League prospects in the Virginia League back in 1920 (Traynor with the Portsmouth Truckers and Holmes with the Richmond Colts). A dead ball era baseball reunion ensued in which Holmes and Traynor reminisced about their Minor League days playing against each other. During the reunion, Traynor took a shining to the younger Holmes and appointed him to be the Pirates bat boy for the game that afternoon. After walking around downtown to get early lunches, the Pirates players all returned to the hotel to get a few hours rest before reporting to Berkshire Park at around 3:30 to begin pre-game warm ups for their 4:30 game.

According to former Gloversville resident James Armstrong (who himself would one day go on to play professionally), "we were extremely excited to be going to our local ballpark to see a Major League Team. As we stood near the home plate backstop to check out our baseball heroes, 'Holmesy' (Jack Holmes) walks by us with the Pirates Team as their bat boy and tipped his hat at us. We all erupted wondering how our buddy got on the field. We were excited for him." As the Glovers players prepared for the game, their ace pitchers Whitey Tulacz and Albert (Duke) Farrington were on the sidelines warming up. Farrington once told me the story of how while he was warming up, an old man wearing a Pirates uniform walked up to him and said "I see that high hard stuff you're throwing 'lefty', throw it to the Waner Boys (Lloyd and Paul), they won't be able to resist it, and they won't be able to touch it. As he walked away, I remember thinking he had the longest arms I had ever seen. Turns out, that old man was the great Honus Wagner." Wagner was a former Pirates player (1897 to 1921), and was at the time their first base coach. It was Wagner's second visit to Gloversville for a baseball game, as he had played an exhibition game himself as the shortstop for the Pittsburgh Nationals when they came to A., J. & G. Park / Parkhurst Field 30 year's prior back on July 24, 1907. When asked what he thought of Gloversville compared to his last trip there, Wagner remarked "the town hasn't changed that much".

Pittsburgh was one of the few Major League outfits that were noted for putting as much into an exhibition as it put into a championship big league game and they used their regular line up to try to win any game (even exhibitions) at any cost. True to form, on the field that day for the Pirates would be 4 future hall of famers; Pie Traynor

45

(Manager-inducted in 1948), Lloyd Waner (CF; inducted in 1967), Paul Waner (RF; inducted in 1952) and Honus Wagner (coach; inducted in Inaugural 1936 Class). A fifth future Hall of Famer Arkie Vaughn (SS; inducted in 1985) was with the team, but sat out of the line-up that day. Also on the field that day was Gloversville resident and former New York Giant star outfielder (1911-21) George J. Burns. Burns was in a Glovers uniform and served as a base coach for the Glovers for the game.

The Pirates dugout was located on the third base side of the field and rather than walk across the field to the Pirates dugout between innings, Wagner would spend the half innings when the Pirates were in the field over at the scoreboard that was located on the first base side of the outfield. Manning the scoreboard that day (and for the entire 1937 season) was Gloversville resident Michael Geraghty. According to Geraghty, "Wagner came and sat with me between innings. Our discussion all afternoon involved talking about his early playing days and the rules of the game that were different. I asked him how much harder it was to hit when the pitching mound was only 50' away from home plate. Wagner told me it was much harder, as the ball was to you and by you in the blink of an eye. Hitting seemed easy after they moved the mound to 60' 6" in 1906. It was a wonderful conversation and Wagner kept referring to me as 'son'. "

More than 2,000 fans attended the game and were delighted to see their hometown Glovers beat the 1909 and 1925 World Champions by a score of 11-8. Whitey Tulacz pitched a complete game gem and was backed up by timely hitting from his team. In the 8th inning of the closely played game, the Glovers hit three consecutive home runs (something never done before or after in the franchise's history) to stun the Major League visitors. And within minutes of the last out, the Pirates were back on a train and headed home to Forbes Field in Pittsburgh to resume their regular season against the Philadelphia Phillies the following day. As the sun set on Berkshire Park that evening, both the Glovers players & fans alike were left wondering 'did we really just beat a Major League team'?

A special dedication ceremony took place on weekend August 5 2017 to place a historical base marker inside of the Runnings Supply Store at the spot where 2B once sat at the former Berkshire Park / Glovers Park. The Marker denotes this historic event and the history of Glovers Baseball on the grounds. On hand to help dedicate the

Marker was former Gloversville Glover (1951) Ralph Vitti (aka Michael Dante).

Author's Note: I would like to give a special thanks to my dear friend Attorney Michael Geraghty who provided much of the history and inspiration for this and many of the stories that I write. He was a walking-talking encyclopedia of sports history (local & national) and a true asset to Gloversville.

Front row—Albert J.Farrington, William Church, John Tulacz, Francis C. Boden, Joseph Petrella, Guy Shatzer, Davies(Mascot). Back row—George Pepper, Kenny Hill, H.Hust, Michael H.Spetrick, Harold Klinkert, Oren Baker, A.Martin(Mgr.). Cunningham,Photo.
GLOVERSVILLE CLUB—CANADIAN-AMERICAN LEAGUE.

1937 Gloversville Glovers team picture.

Glovers Park aerial photograph.

A 4347 Kingsborough Hotel, Gloversville, N. Y.

Monday.

In town this A.M. shaking hands with trade. Am blessed with "prospects."

Geo.

49

The Integration of Professional Baseball
had roots in Fulton County

"GLOVERS WILL HAVE NEGRO IN OUTFIELD" was the headline on the sports page in the Gloversville/Johnstown Leader-Republic on July 19, 1947. As jolting as such a headline sounds, the city of Gloversville was actually trend-setting in helping the efforts of the integration of modern day professional baseball.

Just three months earlier, Jackie Robinson had broken the color barrier in Major League Baseball when he made his debut for the Brooklyn Dodgers. Robinson's trek to the big leagues started when team owner Branch Rickey signed him to a professional contract with the Brooklyn Dodgers in the fall of 1945. This signing blatantly broke the informal color line that baseball had lived under since 1899, which did not allow black players to play professional baseball at any level. Robinson spent the 1946 season with the Montreal Royals of the International League (Dodgers AAA affiliate in Quebec Ontario).

After spending one season with Montreal where he batted .349 and stole 40 bases, Robinson made his historic Major League debut on April 15, 1947 for the Brooklyn Dodgers. The event not only changed professional baseball, but all sports and widespread civil rights.

Less than three months later, the Cleveland Indians would follow the Dodgers lead when owner Bill Veeck also signed a black player named Lawrence "Larry" Doby to a contract on July 3rd. Doby would bypass the minor leagues and would play his first professional game for the Indians on July 5, 1947. In doing so, he became the second black in Major League Baseball and the first to play in the American League. One week later, the St. Louis Browns (forerunner to the Baltimore Orioles) would become the third Major League organization to sign a black player when they penned contracts with Negro Leaguers Hank Thompson, Willard Brown and Piper Davis. A fourth black signed that same day by the Browns was a college player from the University of Toledo named Charlie "Chuck" Harmon. Both Thompson and Brown would be assigned to the Brown's Major League roster (making their MLB debuts on July 17th & 18th), and Davis would stay with the Negro League Birmingham Black Barons (team they signed him from), and kept as an 'option' to the Browns. With no more spots on the roster available on the Major League team, the Browns were left with the arduous task of finding a minor league team/town willing to take Harmon.

Like Robinson, Harmon was college educated, an all-around gifted athlete (starred in both basketball & baseball at Toledo) and had military service. In fact, while stationed at the Great Lakes Illinois Naval Center during WWII (1943-45) he was a teammate of Larry Doby on the Navy baseball team. However, integration of Major League sports was less than 100 days old, and the task of finding a team for even an all-around quality person like Harmon was still near impossible. From 1942-49, the Browns had a minor-league affiliation with the Class C Gloversville Glovers of the Canadian-American League. The Browns sent a telegraphic wire to the Glovers management asking if the club would accept a Negro. Glovers President Harry F. Dunkel's wire response back was that they would, provided that the ball player was good enough to really help the team.

It is no surprise to me that Gloversville would have no issue accepting a black playing for them as the area had welcomed Negro teams (aka Cuban Teams) to play numerous exhibition games at Parkhurst Field and Darling Field during the 1910's through the 30's. The Glovers themselves had played in exhibition games against black teams in 1937 when they took on the Albany Black Sox and the Schenectady Mohawk Colored Giants. Such games between professional white teams and black teams were not very commonplace in the 1930's.

Harmon remembers being warmly welcomed in Gloversville by both his teammates and the fans. In a 2003 interview with Leader-Herald Sports Writer James Ellis, Harmon spoke of how Gloversville businessman Hal Sutliff (Gloversville Sport Shop) was at the train station in Fonda awaiting his arrival in July 1947 and drove him to Gloversville. This gesture was the start of a life-long friendship, and Sutliff's Sport Shop sporting goods store would end up providing Harmon with any baseball equipment he needed for his entire professional career. Harmon spent the rest of the 1947 season with the Glovers and met his future wife Daurel Woodley. The two were married a few months after the season ended and would enjoy 61 years of marriage and raise 3 children together. After taking the 1948 season off to complete his college studies at the University of Toledo, Harmon returned to the Glovers for most of the 1949 season, and resided in Gloversville for the next several years.

The Glovers would continue to sign black ballplayers in the last two years of their existence. In 1950, they enlisted the services of black outfielder Harry Wilson. They would sign two more blacks in 1951 when they brought in pitcher Walter James and shortstop Pedro Arroyo. At the time the Canadian-American League folded in 1951, fellow league members the Amsterdam Rugmakers (New York Yankees), the Schenectady Blue Jays (Philadelphia Phillies), and the Oneonta Red Sox (Boston Red Sox) never integrated, nor did their parent clubs. The Red Sox would eventually become the last Major League team to integrate on July 21, 1959 when they brought in Pumpsie Green. This was almost 12 years to the day after Gloversville had allowed Harmon to take the field at Glovers Park back on July 19, 1947.

After six seasons in the minor leagues, Harmon would eventually go onto become the first African American to play for the Cincinnati Reds on April 17, 1954. He would enjoy four seasons in the Major Leagues with the Reds, St. Louis Cardinals and Philadelphia Phillies, and several seasons after that as a scout for the Cleveland Indians and Atlanta Braves.

Today, at age 93, Harmon resides in Golf Manor OH (suburb of Cincinnati), which has a street "Chuck Harmon Way" named in his honor. Many other accolades have been bestowed upon this former Gloversville Glover and one time Gloversville resident for his role in helping integrate professional baseball. He threw out the very first pitch to Hall of Famer Barry Larkin in the first exhibition game at the Cincinnati Red's Great American Ballpark on March 28, 2003. In 2004, in celebration of the 50th Anniversary of Harmon becoming the first African American to play for the Reds, a plaque with Harmon's image and accomplishments was mounted near the entrance to Great American Ball Park. At the 2009 Major League Baseball Civil Rights Game in Cincinnati, Harmon was honored by former President Bill Clinton in his speech. At the 2010 Civil Rights Game in Cincinnati, the day was also called "Chuck Harmon Day" and the Reds gave away 30,000 number "10" Harmon jerseys. One of those jerseys (signed by Harmon) is on display at the Fulton County Museum's "History of baseball in Fulton County Timeline Display". Harmon was inducted into the Fulton County Baseball & Sports Hall of Fame at the August 2014 Vintage Baseball Game at Parkhurst Field in Gloversville. And in July 2015, a life size statue of Harmon was unveiled at the entrance to the P&G Cincinnati Major League Baseball Youth Academy Complex in Cincinnati as part of the 2015 MLB All-Star Game.

Branch Rickey, Jackie Robinson, Bill Veeck and Larry Doby have also been recognized by Major League Baseball for their roles in integrating professional baseball with enshrinement into the Cooperstown Baseball Hall of Fame. Cities like Montreal and Gloversville should also be lauded for being open minded enough to care more about the talent of an individual, rather than the color of their skin in a time when hatred and bigotry was not only tolerated, but was the norm. To look back now 70 years later, it is amazing to think that the city of Gloversville supported such a monumental integration effort that has had a lasting impact on professional sports, as well as a profound impact on making the world a more equitable place. I am proud to say I am from Gloversville!

Afterword: Sadly, Chuck Harmon, passed away on March 19, 2019 at the age of 94. At the news of his passing, many tributes were published including the following, *"The entire Reds family is saddened to lose one of its great ambassadors. The first African American to play for the Reds, Chuck Harmon was much more than a ballplayer," said Reds Chief Executive Officer Bob Castellini. "He represents a pivot point in Reds history. Chuck's positive attitude and disposition helped diffuse the adversity he faced, and set the tone for those following in his footsteps. He was beloved by his teammates during his career and remained a treasure to this franchise and its fans throughout his life. He will be missed."*

Rick Walls, Executive Director of the Reds Hall of Fame and Museum, said, *"The Reds Hall of Fame and Museum joins Reds Country in mourning the loss of one of our great icons. Chuck Harmon was a symbol of greatness and inspiration, and his life story will live on forever in the museum, being told countless times to generations of Reds fans."*[14]

According to the Dayton Daily News, in 2007, when Chuck Harmon was asked to comment on being the first black player for the Reds. Harmon replied:

> *"Being the first, I said, 'So I was the first. So what? I'm going to make sure I'm not the last.' That's all I thought about. Being the first? Great. But I watched how I carried myself so I wouldn't negate all the rest of the black ballplayers from getting a chance with the Reds. Don't go out there and act a fool."* [15]

Chuck Harmon while playing with the Gloversville Glovers.

Charles Harmon Baseball Card Flyer.

Chuck Harmon Billboard.

*Chuck Harmon with his family at the Fulton County Hall of Fame
inductions with the "Glovers Park" Historical Roadside Marker.*

Chuck Harmon in front of his monument at P&G Cincinnati, Major League Baseball Youth Academy Complex, in Cincinnati, Ohio. The monument was unveiled as part of the 2015 MLB All-Star Game.

The Cincinnati Reds place a wreath at the Chuck Harmon
monument after he passed away on March 19, 2019.

110th Anniversary of the Greatest Month in Gloversville Baseball History

In the Parkhurst Field documentary trailer created in 2014 (visit www.parkhurstfield.org/get-the-book to view), Parkhurst Field Foundation President David Karpinski refers to "the best month of baseball in any town, let alone Gloversville". He is referring to the period of "July 5, 1907 to July 24, 1907" and the activity that took place at A., J. & G. Park (Parkhurst Field) on Harrison Street in Gloversville 110 years ago this month. During that period, two Major League Teams would stop to play exhibition games at the home of the A., J. & G's, as well as the appearance by one of the most iconic figures in both baseball and Hollywood cinema.

A., J. & G. Park was in just its second season of existence, as the Amsterdam-Johnstown-Gloversville (A., J. & G's, JAGS, Hyphens or Earlites as they were commonly referred to) moved from their previous location at the Johnstown Fairgrounds (area near the intersection of Perry Street & Townsend Avenue in Johnstown) and competed in the old New York State League of Class B professional baseball. The move was prompted by the success of the team having won the New York State League Championship in 1905. On July 12, 1906, the park opened at its new Gloversville location on Harrison Street (now Parkhurst Field / Gloversville Little League) and over the next three seasons would host two Major League teams, as well as more than 70 future & former Major League players who either played for the JAGS or were part of the visiting New York State League teams who came to play them.

Based on the success of attendance during the 1906 season and a professional field that rivaled that of any Major League park at that time, the F., J. & G. Railroad (owners of the JAGS) decided to begin booking Major League Teams who were traveling through the Mohawk Valley in route from games in Boston, going to Major League cities out West. Additional game ticket sales and train fare from fans to get to the park were the motivators. Such exhibition game detours on off/travel days also served as a means for the Major League team owners to help defray the costs of their road trips. Team train fare, hotels and meal costs were recouped as the Big-League clubs received a lump sum appearance fee and/or a percentage of the gate receipts.

59

The historic month of baseball began with the arrival of the Boston Americans (Red Sox) led by player/manager Cy Young on Friday July 5, 1907. The team had just finished a home stand the day before against the Washington Senators and were in route to Detroit for a game with the Tigers scheduled for Saturday July 6th. It was part of a 15-game road trip that would also see them play in Cleveland, St. Louis and Chicago. In 1906 these Major League cities were the westward most destinations of professional baseball and considered the most grueling travel on the players. It is believed that the reason Boston agreed to stop in Gloversville was its close proximity to its first baseman Myron "Moose" Grimshaw's hometown of Canajoharie. It seemed to be a natural gate (financial) bonanza for both the JAGS management and subsequently that of Boston's as it was assumed that all of Grimshaw's family and hometown admirers from Canajoharie and the Mohawk Valley area would come to watch their local hero suit up to play as a professional. At this point in his career, Cy Young had already won 450 of the 511 games he would win over his career and was one of the biggest stars in the game. While he did not pitch that day, he was there with the team in his capacity as their manager. Grimshaw, who normally played first base or the outfield, was at the short stop position for this game. Although he only went 1 for 5 at the plate, one newspaper account stated that "the fielding of Grimshaw at short was worth the price of admission alone". Boston rapped out 10 hits (to the JAGS 8) and easily won the contest by a score of 8-3 leaving the fans of Gloversville thrilled with the experience of having a Major League team come to the area for the very first time in history.

Approximately 20 days later, a second Major League team visited Gloversville when the Pittsburgh Nationals came to Gloversville on July 24th. Pittsburgh had just finished a series in Boston against the Boston Doves and were in route back to Pittsburgh for a series against the Philadelphia Phillies on July 25th. The connection leading to Gloversville securing this Big-League club for an exhibition was the friendship between the JAGS manager Howard Earl and the owner of the Pittsburgh team Barney Dreyfuss. During this period, Dreyfuss was one of the most notable figures in the baseball limelight and had known Earl from his days as a Major Leaguer in the late 1800's. The team arrived in Gloversville at 10am on the morning of the July 24th and were shown the places of interest around town before their afternoon game.

As the Pittsburgh team took the field at A., J. & G. Park that afternoon, they were led by short stop Honus Wagner. Playing in his 11th season in the Big-leagues, Wagner had already banged out 1751 of the 3420 hits he would manufacture over 21 years as a Major Leaguer and would become just the second Major Leaguer to compile 3,000 hits in a career (Cap Anson was the first). Also on the field that day was future Hall of Famer Fred Clark (HOF 1945) who manned left field. Another future Hall of Famer, pitcher Vic Willis (HOF 1995) did not pitch that day, but was with the team as they beat the local A., J. & G's by a score of 5-0. Following the game, Dreyfuss and his team were taken to the Hotel Kingsborough on South Main Street (now the 'Kingsboro' Apartments) where they were dinner guests of JAGS manager Howard Earl and team Secretary Ball.

And if having two Major League clubs in town to play in the same 20-day period is not impressive enough, tucked in between these historic exhibition games, came a three-day stint by one of the most iconic figures in baseball & Hollywood cinema. On Tuesday July 16, 1907, the Scranton Miners of the New York State League came to Gloversville to play a New York State League game against the JAGS. With this team was a 29 year old player by the name of Archibald "Moonlight Doc" Graham who played left field. Graham was the subject of the 1989 Universal Pictures blockbuster baseball drama called "Field of Dreams". The movie featured Kevin Costner, James Earl Jones, Ray Liotta and Burt Lancaster, and centered around a young baseball player named Archie Graham who had one game (half an inning-in the field) with the New York Giants in 1922, but never got an official at bat as a Major Leaguer. In the movie, he quit baseball after that game and became a doctor. Turns out, Graham was a real player who actually did have one game (and no official at bat) with the New York Giants, but in 1905. And he really did become a doctor in Chisolm Minnesota. However, the movie had it backwards, and rather than quitting baseball after that one Big League game, Graham returned to the New York State League as a member of the Scranton Miners team for the 1906 & 1907 seasons, before dedicating the rest of his life to practicing medicine and helping children for more than 50 years.

In the July 16th game at A., J. & G. Park, Graham was hitless in 5 at bats and Scranton won the game 4-3. The July 17th game was rained out, so the JAGS & the Miners played a double header on July 18th.

In the first game, Graham went 1 for 5 and stole a base, while Scranton cruised to a 7-0 win. In the second game, Graham went 1 for 4, stole another base, was hit by a pitch, and scored the only run for Scranton as the JAGS squeaked out a 2-1 win.

Pretty amazing that so much history could have taken place in a small town like Gloversville, let alone having it all packed into a 20-day period. A few of the players involved in these historic games would resurface in Gloversville in the coming years. Grimshaw would return to A., J. & G. Park/Parkhurst Field in 1914 when he played for semi-professional Danforth's Club in the Sunset League and as their player/manager in 1915. Grimshaw was inducted into the Fulton County Baseball & Sports HOF at a Parkhurst Field ceremony in July of 2016. Wagner would return to Gloversville almost 30 years to the day on July 26, 1937 with the Pittsburgh Pirates for yet another exhibition game. This time his playing career was over and he was a charter member of the Baseball Hall of Fame (enshrined with inaugural class of 1936) and was here in the capacity of first base coach. This game was against the Gloversville Glovers (Class C Canadian-American League) and played at Berkshire Park/Glovers Park on Elmwood Avenue (area is now the site of the Runnings Supply Store/Hannaford Grocery Store/House of Pizza Restaurant).

The 110th Anniversary of this historical month in local baseball history was commemorated with a special Vintage Baseball Game on August 6, 2017 at Parkhurst Field in Gloversville. The Whately Pioneers of Western Massachusetts faced the A., J. & G's of Fulton County in a match of baseball played by the rules of Major League Baseball from 1886. Both teams wore period authentic uniforms and played utilizing period specific equipment (balls, bats & gloves). The A., J. & G's wore replica jerseys of what the JAGS wore 110 years prior during the 1907 season. During the event, former 1951 Gloversville Glover Ralph Vitti/aka Hollywood actor Michael Dante was inducted into the Fulton County Baseball & Sports Hall of Fame. He also was the Manager of the A., J. & G. team for the Vintage Game. More details about the Vintage Game and the full history of A., J. & G. Park/Parkhurst Field can be viewed at www.parkhurstfield.org or visit the Facebook page "Parkhurst Field".

1907 Pirates team picture.

Cy Young in 1903.

Moonlight "Doc" Graham in his Scranton Miners uniform.

SNAPPY PLAYS
DELIGHT CROWD

Boston Americans Took the
Game, But It Was a Joy to
See Them Play Ball,
In Any Event.

A. J. & G.

	AB.	R.	H.	P.	A.	E.
Barry, 3b	4	0	1	1	0	1
Leard, ss	4	0	0	4	4	1
McCormack, lf	4	0	0	1	0	0
Weaver, cf	4	1	1	4	0	0
Reardon, rf	4	0	2	0	0	0
Earl, 1b	2	0	0	12	1	1
Childs, 2b	4	1	1	1	2	0
Coorey, c	4	1	2	4	0	1
Purcell, p	4	0	1	0	6	1
McNeal, *	1	0	0	0	0	0
Totals	31	3	8	27	13	5

BOSTON.

	AB.	R.	H.	P.	A.	E.
Sullivan, cf	4	1	3	3	0	0
Grimshaw, ss	5	0	1	0	5	0
Knight, 3b	5	0	1	1	1	0
Ferris, 2b	5	0	1	1	3	0
Unglaub, 1b	3	2	1	12	1	1
Armbruster, c	4	1	0	4	0	0
Glaze, lf	4	2	3	3	0	0
Jacobson, rf	4	1	0	2	0	0
Oberlin, p	4	1	1	1	4	0
Totals	38	8	10	27	14	1

*Batted for Earl in the ninth.

Score by innings:

A.-J.-G. .... 0 0 1 0 0 1 1 0 0—3
Boston .... 0 4 0 2 0 0 0 1 1—8

SUMMARY.

Two base hits—Weaver, Reardon, Sullivan.

Three base hit—Child.

Home run—Sullivan.

Sacrifice hits—Sullivan, Unglaub.

Stolen bases—Barry, Knight, Ferris.

Left on bases—A.-J.-G., 6; Boston 4.

First base on balls—Off Purcell 1.

First base on errors—Boston 4.

Struck out—By Purcell 3; By Oberlin 3.

Passed balls—Armbruster.

Wild pitches—Purcell 2.

Hit by pitcher—Earl, by Oberlin.

Time—1:35.

Umpire—Callahan.

1907 Box Score.

65

Vintage Baseball in Fulton County

The game of baseball dates back to 1839 when Abner Doubleday is credited with having laid out the first version of the game on Eli Phinney's cow pasture in Cooperstown New York. While the same premises of the game laid out in 1839 have lasted the test of time, many rule changes have taken place over the 175+ years since.

Today, groups of baseball historians & enthusiasts put together "Vintage Games" which employee the rules & equipment of specific periods of professional baseball. These games can be likened to what "war re-enactors" do when they recreate specific military battles. Like re-enactments, the players are dressed in period reproduction uniforms and utilize period authentic equipment. The main difference though, is that Vintage Baseball Games are real games. These games take place at open-air museums, living history villages and city parks in over two dozen states across the United States.

For the last few years, such games (matches) have taken place at Parkhurst Field (Gloversville Little League) on Harrison Street in Gloversville. These particular games are played utilizing the rules of Major League Baseball employed in 1886.

The Rules:
In 1886 era Vintage Baseball, the same size diamond is used, except there is no pitcher's mound. Pitchers instead throw from a 4' by 6' box with the front of the box just 50' from home plate. The pitcher can fake a throw to any base except home. Faking to home would be the only time a balk is called. There are still three strikes for an out, but 7 balls equal a walk (not 4). A batter being hit by a pitch is considered only a "ball" and the batter cannot take a base. Foul balls do not count as strikes and any ball hit by a batter (even a tick) that is caught by the catcher is an out, even on the first pitch of any at bat. Any dropped 3rd strike forces all runners to try to advance to the next base, even if bases are loaded. In fact, if a catcher drops a 3rd strike with bases loaded, he can pick up the ball and step on home plate for an out, because the runner on third is forced to go. When a hitter approaches the plate, he must inform the umpire which "zone" he is requesting. A "high zone" is from the waist to the shoulders. A "low zone" is from the bottom of the knee to the waist. A pitcher must then throw within the "called zone" for it to be called

a strike. There is no Infield Fly Rule and a fielder can purposely drop a fly ball to start a double play.

The Equipment:
The bats are wooden and the gloves used in the games would barely pass as a gardening glove or driving glove today. They have very little padding, no laces and no webbing between the thumb and fore finger. No batting helmets are used, and the ball is a bit larger than a modern baseball, is sewn in quarters and not wound as tight (less flight).

Some Vintage Baseball Terms:
Match = Game
Club Nine = Team
Sir = Umpire
Cranks = Fans
Captain = Manager
Frames = Innings
Tally Keeper = Score Keeper
Ballist = Player
Striker = Batter
Hurler = Pitcher
First Keeper = First Baseman
Behind = Catcher
Horse Hide/Onion = Ball
Willow = Bat
Striker to the Line = Batter Up
Dish = Home Plate
Four Baser = Home Run
Ace/Tally = Run
Hurl = Throw/Pitch
Foul Tick = Foul Ball
Player Dead = Out
Muff = Error
Leg It = Run to the Base
Show a Little Ginger = Play Harder
Stir Your Stumps = Play Harder
Huzzah! = Hurray

To experience a Vintage Game for yourself, the next Parkhurst Field Vintage Game will be taking place today at 1pm. It will be part of the Fulton County Baseball & Sports Hall of Fame inductions. Set to square off are the Whately Pioneers of Western Massachusetts and the A., J. & G's of Upstate New York. The A., J. & G's (JAGS) are a squad of local former Amsterdam, Johnstown and Gloversville Little Leaguers (now grown men). The local JAGS squad will be wearing commemorative A., J. & G uniforms that match those that the team wore 110 years ago when A., J. & G Park (Parkhurst Field) was in its professional hey-day in 1907. At 11am, a warm-up game will take place between the Gloversville Little League All-Stars, wearing Gloversville Glovers throw-back uniforms, against the Johnstown Little League All-Stars wearing Johnstown Buckskins throw-back uniforms. At 12:30, the Fulton County Baseball & Sports Hall of Fame will be inducting 1951 Gloversville Glover Michael Dante. Dante played for the Glovers in 1951 as Ralph Vitti, before becoming a Hollywood actor under the stage name of Michael Dante. Dante, who is credited with roles in nearly 30 Hollywood films and 150 television shows, will be in attendance and serve as the JAGS manager for the contest. The game & inductions will also be part of the Parkhurst Field Foundations fundraiser for the "Field of Dreams Capital Campaign" that will be broadcast live on WIZR 102.9 FM and 930 AM from 9am to 4pm. Former area Little Leaguers, coaches and parents will be on the air throughout the day sharing their memories of Parkhurst Field. Admission to the event is FREE. If you are unable to attend, but would like to make a donation to the campaign, you can text 2017VINTAGE to 71777 with a pledge or go to www.parkhurstfield.org. You can also mail donations to PO Box 706, Gloversville, NY 12078. The goal of the event is to raise $50,000 towards the campaign goal of $2.3M.

A.-J.-G. Team, 1907.
MANNING, Photographer, Utica.

1907 "A-J-G" Baseball Team.

*Andy Fusco and Al Busch during the 2012 Vintage Baseball Game
at Parkhurst Field in Gloversville, NY.*

Generations mirror each other at Parkhurst Field

In 1907, the Pittsburgh Pirates made their first appearance in the Fulton County area when they played an exhibition game at A., J. & G Park / Parkhurst Field on July 24, 1907. The game was against the A., J. & G's of the New York State League, and was the result of a long-time friendship between Pittsburgh Pirates owner Barney Dreyfuss and the A., J. & G manager Howard Earl (former Major League Player). The pair set up the game to fill in a travel day (and help defray the teams travel expenses) for the Pirates as they traveled from their July 23rd game in Boston against the Boston Doves, and were in route back to Pittsburgh for a series against the Philadelphia Phillies beginning on July 25th.

The Pirates team was led by future baseball hall of famer Honus Wagner, who at the time was 33 years old and in the prime of his Hall of Fame career (11th season). Also on that team was Albany native Edward Jaykill Phelps. Phelps, a catcher, was born in Albany in 1879 and after playing school ball for Albany High School, began playing professionally at the age of 19 for the Danbury Hatters of the Connecticut State League. After 4 seasons with various teams in the minor leagues, his contract was purchased by Pittsburgh Pirates owner Barney Dreyfuss from the Rochester Bronchos of the Eastern League in 1902.

Phelps was considered a very good catcher who could hit, throw and run the bases with speed. He would help the Pirates win the 1902 and 1903 National League Pennants and played in the 1903 World Series against the Boston Americans and Cy Young. 1903 marked the first modern World Series pitting the top team from the American League going up against the top team from the National League for a best of 9 games championship series. Boston would win the series 5 games to 3, and Phelps claim to fame would become that he was the first National League catcher in the history of the World Series, as he was behind the plate for the Pirates in all 8 games.

Phelps is also known for the "Phelps Decision" that took place in 1906. After the 1904 season, Phelps was traded in February 1905 to the Cincinnati Reds. He would spend the entire 1905 season as the back-up catcher for the Reds, playing in 44 games and batting .231 . In mid-May of the 1906 season, Reds owner August "Garry"

Herrmann (who was also the chairman of the National Baseball Commission) asked waivers on Phelps. But before the 10-day waiver period had expired, Herrmann sold Phelps to the Boston Pilgrims of the American League. On the tenth day of the waiver period, Phelps signed contract with Barney Dreyfuss to go back to the Pirates. Although the Pirates already had two catchers, Dreyfuss knew Phelps could hit and run well, so tried to being him back to fill the pinch hitter role for his club. However, this caused a debate over who owned the rights to Phelps; Boston or Pittsburgh. With the National Agreement of 1903, which brought peace between the veteran National League and the fledgling American League, a 3-person governing body of Major League Baseball was created called the National Commission. The Commission was made up of the American League President (Ban Johnson in 1903), the National League President (Harry Pulliam in 1903) and a Chairperson to make the ultimate decisions on any debates pertaining to the league. Because of his instrumental role in brokering the peace accord between the two leagues in 1903, Reds owner Herrmann was named the chairman. Under the rules of the commission, the chairman (Herrmann) had absolute power in the resolution of contractual claims & disputes. In the Phelps situation, Herrmann ruled in favor of Boston, claiming that Phelps had given him permission to sell his contract to the Boston Pilgrims. Phelps was adamant that he had not given Herrmann permission to sell his contract. Herrmann was also steadfast to his version of the situation and held to his decision that Phelps' contract would remain with the Boston club. Pirate's owner Barney Dreyfuss, who had always been outspoken in his belief that as a team owner, Herrmann should not hold the position of leading the commission and making decisions that could favor his own team. A week later, Dreyfuss brought to light that he had a source who claimed that Herrmann had wagered $6,000 that the Pirates would not win the 1906 National League Pennant. Herrmann did not deny the alleged wager, but claimed that it had been made in jest, after a night of drinking. Caught in a very difficult position, Herrmann reversed his decision and awarded Phelps' contract to Dreyfuss and he went back to the Pirates. This was the first time that the National Commission had been placed in such an awkward position. It would not be the last and such conflicts of interest of an owner also heading up the governing body of Major League Baseball would taint the sport until the Black Sox scandal of the 1919 World Series eventually brought the commission down. The scandal would lead to the creation of a full time Commissioner of Baseball position in 1920, when non-baseball figure and Federal Judge Kenesaw Mountain Landis was hired to clean up the game and restore public faith in America's national pastime.

Phelps career as a Major Leaguer would last through 1913 and he would also play for the St. Louis Cardinals and the Brooklyn Dodgers. After 11 seasons in the Major Leagues, he returned home to upstate New York be the player/manager of the Albany Senators in the New York State League in 1914 and 915. In 1931, Phelps, along with fellow area ex-Major Leaguer Matty Fitzgerald, would be back involved in high level baseball as commissioners of the Albany Twilight League that was formed at Bleecker Stadium in Albany. The league, which is still in existence today, featured the best amateur players in Upstate New York.

Phelps would make his last public baseball appearance at Shuttleworth Park in Amsterdam in 1939. It was for "George Burns Day" at the park that was honoring Gloversville resident and former Major Leaguer George Burns, who had a 15-year career in the Big Leagues with the New York Giants, Cincinnati Reds and Philadelphia Phillies. Phelps, along with 6 other former Major Leaguers from the Capital District were in attendance for the event.

Phelps died in East Greenbush New York in 1942 at the age of 62, and is buried in the Greenbush Reformed Cemetery. While it has been 75 years since his death, the Phelps name was recently heard over the public-address system at Parkhurst Field a few weeks ago during their annual Vintage Baseball Game. The game featured a matchup between the Whately Pioneers of Western Massachusetts and the A., J. & G's of Fulton County. The game was played by the rules of MLB from 1886 and the players wore throwback uniforms and played utilizing period authentic equipment.

The local A., J. & G. team is traditionally made up of former local Little Leaguers from Amsterdam-Johnstown-Gloversville (A., J. & G's), but this year's team welcomed a duo from Troy New York who brought back a nostalgic piece of the parks history 110 years after Ed Phelps and the Pittsburgh Pirates played there in 1907. The duo was Jim Phelps and his son Colby; the Great Grandson and Great-Great Grandson of Ed Phelps. Several months prior to the event, the elder Phelps had reached out to a board member of the

Parkhurst Field Foundation about his Great Grandfather's connection to the park. The two Phelps descendants were then asked to get take part in the game. The youngest Phelps (Colby) took on the role of A., J. & G. bat boy, while the elder Phelps suited up to play. Ironically, Colby's middle name is "Jaykill", which was given to him as a tribute to his Great-Great Grandfather who had the same middle name. According to his Father, "Colby definitely has the Phelps baseball gene; he is good at it (is 13 and plays on the Brunswick Buckeyes Travel Team), has a great passion for the game, and is very much in-tune with his (middle) name sakes career."

Jim (presently a Rensselaer County Sheriff) played baseball for Columbia HS growing up and on local travel teams. Other than pick up softball games and throwing batting practice to his son Colby's youth travel teams, Jim had not played in an organized baseball game since enlisting in the Air Force more than 25 years ago. Despite the long lay-off from the game, the "Phelps baseball gene" showed up during the game, as Jim went 2-4, driving in 2 runs and scoring one as the A., J. & G's defeated the Pioneers by a score of 15 to 8.

After the game, the Phelps family reflected on what the day meant to his family. According to Jim, *"It was our 'Field of Dreams' moment! We were on the same field that that he (Grandfather Ed Phelps) played on 110 years earlier. To do that alone would have been fantastic, but to do that with my son was magical. And to have both of us put those jerseys on (replica 1907 A., J. & G uniforms), it felt like we had stepped back in time into that era. To see that smile on Colb's face, I knew there was a heavenly connection that day. I could never ask for anything more. After the game, when Dave Karpinski took me over to the spot where the marker is for the original field and said 'this is the spot where your Grandfather crouched and caught during that game in 1907', I got goose bumps and a lump in my throat. And I could see it in my son's eyes that he was awestruck as well. It was definitely our families 'Field of Dreams' moment."*

Photos and game used equipment from both this year's Vintage Game and the historic visit by Ed Phelps and the Pittsburgh Pirates in 1907 are on display at the Parkhurst Field Museum located on premises at Parkhurst Field (50 Harrison Street in Gloversville).

Phelps as a Cincinnati Red.

Phelps as a Brooklyn Dodger.

Colby and Jim Phelps at the 2017 Vintage Baseball Game at Parkhurst Field in Gloversville, NY.

Foster, Sanford and baseball with a Flair

If you attended school in either Gloversville or Mayfield between the 1960's and the 1990's, chances are you crossed paths with Physical Education instructors Jack Sanford or Tom Foster. Both men grew up in Gloversville and were two of the most gifted athletes to come out of the Upstate New York area in the early 1950's.

Jack Sanford, a 1951 graduate of Gloversville High School, was the team's leader on legendary Gloversville High School Coach Duke Millers infamous 1951 undefeated baseball team. After a very successful high school career in which he starred in football (one of the best passers in the Capital District), basketball (1950/51 Captain of the Jack Kobuskie's Reindeer Five) and baseball (drawing dozens of Major League Scouts to local high school games to recruit him), Sanford took his talents on to play college baseball. After one semester at Ithaca College (Ithaca NY) in the Fall of 1951, he transferred to Springfield College (Springfield MA) for the Spring 1952 semester. Because of the transfer, he was not allowed to pitch that season. However, he would make up for that lost season by winning the first 6 games of his rookie college season as a sophomore and compiled a 19-3 pitching record for Springfield over three seasons. This record was considered one of the best three-year records in all of college baseball and helped lead the Springfield Team to the College World Series in Omaha Nebraska in 1955. During the summers, he and fellow Gloversville baseball star Joe Kobuskie (also on the Springfield team) played in Canada for the Maine-New Brunswick Team in Grand Falls New Brunswick (a league similar to the Perfect Game League in which the Amsterdam Mohawks participate in each summer).

After graduating from Springfield College with a Bachelor of Science Degree in Health & Physical Education in the spring of 1955, he was signed to a professional baseball contract with the Pittsburgh Pirates by baseball Hall of Famer Branch Rickey (Rickey also signed Jackie Robinson to a contract in 1947). His first season was spent with the Williamsport Grays (Williamsport PA) of the Eastern League, where he was a teammate of 18-year old prospect Bill Mazeroski. Mazeroski would go on the World Series fame with his walk off home run in Game 7 of the 1960 World Series against the New York Yankees and eventually be inducted into the National Baseball Hall of Fame in 2001. The 1956 campaign saw Sanford back at Williamsport where he was the teams pitching work horse, winning 8 games, while appearing in 33 games (23 starts & 10 relief appearances). It was that same year that he married Williamsport native Diane Bixler. He was then signed by the St. Louis Cardinals organization in 1957 and pitched for the Jacksonville Braves (Jacksonville FL) of the South Atlantic League that year. In 1958 he split time with the New York White Roses (York PA) of the Eastern League and then back in the Pirates organization with the Lincoln Chiefs of the Western League in Lincoln Nebraska. Calcium deposits on his pitching elbow caused him to leave baseball after the 1958 season.

The Sanford's returned to Upstate New York to start a family and Jack began his teaching career as a physical education teacher for the Speculator School District beginning in the fall of 1958 through 1962. While Speculator did not have sports teams of their own, he spent those years as an assistant coach for the Wells High School basketball team under Jack Belmont. Belmont was also a well-known baseball coach in the area, and Sanford spent his high school summers playing for Belmont's infamous semi-pro town teams. Sanford then took a position with the Mayfield School District in 1962 to teach, as well as coach. There, he coached several boys & girls sports, including Soccer, Track, Gymnastics, and Basketball & Baseball. During the summers, he and his family (children; Jack, Jeff, Mark and Mandy) returned to Diane's hometown of Williamsport Pennsylvania where Jack served as the director of Little League International's Baseball Camps and was known in the Little League circles nationally as an authority on pitching instruction. According to Sanford, "I was recruited to get involved at Little League International by my Springfield College Professor of Kinesiology, Dr. Creighton J. Hale. Hale left Springfield to join that organization to promote player safety and eventually became the President and Chief Executive of Little League International." Hale is credited with bringing many safety measures to the game, including creating and patenting the hard-plastic full head batting helmet with interior padding and ear flaps that is now used at all levels of the game. In later years, Sanford would spend summers locally promoting and instructing camps for gymnastics, basketball and baseball, including the popular Tri-County Baseball Camps (with Roger Gifford & Craig Phillips) at Parkhurst Field in Gloversville each summer.

77

Tom Foster took a different route to the professional ranks by first taking a shot at Football. At the age of 16, his pitching skills caught the attention of the Brooklyn Dodgers and the New York Giants, who both offered him professional contracts. However, Foster's Mother (Winifred) forbid him from signing professionally until he graduated from high school. He left Gloversville High School in 1953 to attend New York Military Academy at Cornwall-on-the-Hudson on a Football scholarship to finish his high school studies. In addition to quarterbacking the football team to an undefeated season, he also excelled in baseball. He was voted the Academy's 1954 MVP with an 18-2 pitching record (he pitched nearly every game that season) and continued to catch the interest of professional baseball scouts. He enrolled at St. Lawrence University in the fall of 1954, but never competed athletically because he was signed to a professional contract by the St. Louis Cardinals in August 1954. He would spend the next two seasons (1955-56) playing Class D level minor league baseball. In 1955, he pitched for the Johnson City Cardinals (Johnson City TN)) in the Appalachian League and the Hamilton Cardinals (Hamilton Ontario) in the Pennsylvania-Ontario-New York League where he helped lead them to the league's championship with a team record of 82-43. The 1956 campaign saw him split time with the Hazlehurst-Baxley Tigers (Hazlehurst GA) of the Georgia State League, as well as the Dothan Cardinals (Dothan AL) of the Alabama-Florida League. After the completion of the 1956 season, he voluntarily enlisted in the United States Army. When the base commander learned of his baseball talents while stationed at Fort Knox in Kentucky, he was recruited to play for the All-Army baseball team. They played 130 game seasons against other base teams across the country. The 1957 team was made up of 18 players, of which 16 had either played professionally, or would go on to play professionally including their first baseman Bill White. White would become a prominent figure in professional baseball as a long-time Major League player (1956, 1958-69), New York Yankee commentator (1971-88 with Phil Rizzuto and Bill Messer) and National League President (1989-94). In White's autobiography "Uppity: My Untold Stories About The Games People Play", he talks about an incident during the 1957 season in which he was not allowed service when the team entered a diner after a game at Fort Leonard Wood in Missouri because he was black. While most of the team stayed at the diner to eat, White talks with great respect about just a few players who stood by his side and left to go find a different place to eat with him, and Foster was one of those players. According to Foster, "I remember the incident well. The owner pulled out a sawed-off shotgun on White and made him leave. A few of us refused to stay and left with White." Because of the lack of support from the entire team, White refused to play with them for the 1958 season. He did finish out the season and they played in the 1957 All-Army tournament against a team from Fort Carson in Colorado that included former Negro League player and future country-western star Charley Pride. Foster would finish out his military service in 1958 and had a 9-0 pitching record for the base team. That same season, he married his wife (Mary Saunders) and they started their family. He returned to professional baseball for one more season in 1959, back with the Dothan Cardinals in the Alabama-Florida League.

Having started a family (he and Mary would have 7 children; Tom, Tim, Margie, Mary, Anne, Elizabeth and Rosanne) he decided to hang up his baseball spikes after the 1959 season and focus on obtaining his college education. In 1962 he graduated with a Bachelor's Degree in Health & Physical Education from the State University of New York at Brockport and a Master's Degree from Ithaca College in 1967. He initially went to work as a Physical Education instructor at the Waterford School District where he got his first taste of coaching, leading the varsity basketball team to the Sectionals. When Duke Miller retired in 1966 as the Gloversville Enlarged School District Physical Education director, long-time instructor Jim Bigsby took over his role. As part of that transition, Miller brought Foster back to Gloversville to fill Bigsby's position as a Physical Education instructor at the Elementary School level and to coach JV football, basketball and baseball. Early in his teaching career, Foster joined Sanford in Williamsport during the summer to also teach pitching at the Little League International Baseball Camps.

In the early 1970's Foster became involved with the F-M Flairs Gymnastics program when his daughters began to train as gymnasts. According to his Daughter Margie Foster-Cunningham (currently the head gymnastics coach at Division I George Washington University), "while he previously knew nothing about the sport, he taught himself the fundamentals and applied the same principles that he himself did as an athlete to train us to be successful." He also called upon Sanford to help him coach. While Sanford did not have any children in the program, he agreed to help. Together, they took over the program and helped train hundreds of gymnasts to successfully compete at a high level, drawing the interest of major college gymnastic programs from across the country. Dozens of those athletes would go on to earn scholarships at the Division I college level, including Foster's daughter Margie who was a five-time All-American at Division I Penn State and part of their 1980 National Championship Team. The F-M Flairs gymnastics program and it members will be the subject of future articles.

Today (2018), at the age of 84, Sanford (retired from teaching at Mayfield in 1999) resides in Mayfield with his wife Diane during the summer and in Florida each winter. Foster, now age 82 (retired from teaching in 1996), resides in Pecks Lake during the summer and in the Washington D.C. area each winter near three of his daughters. Both Sanford & Foster were inducted into the Fulton County Baseball & Sports Hall of Fame on August 11, 2018 at Parkhurst Field in Gloversville New York. They were honored for both their professional playing careers, as well as their role in developing the areas female athletes into collegiate gymnasts.

JACK SANFORD, Gloversville, star hurler for Springfield College, last night signed a contract with Pittsburgh in the National League.

Jack Sanford in 1955.

Tom Foster.

Tom Foster.

Sanford and Foster spotting on vault.

Flairs Foster and Sanford.

The Death & Rebirth of an economy at the Ballpark

At the turn of the 20th century, the leather and glove industries of Fulton County dominated the Upstate New York economy. At its peak, several hundred glove shops and ancillary businesses tied to this industry dotted Fulton County, providing jobs to anyone willing to work and stabilized the local economy.

At the forefront of these industries was Sexton Northrup, who was a senior member of the well-known Northrup Glove Manufacturing Company that was headquartered in Johnstown. He was a pioneer of the glove manufacturing business in the late 1800's/early 1900's and his knowledge of leather and glove making was authoritative.

He was born in Broadalbin in 1844, where he was raised and schooled. His father (James) and his uncle (J.N. Richards) formed a co-partnership in the glove business in the early 1860's, which became one of the largest in Fulton County. He worked for them as a young boy, eventually becoming their general manager. Sexton set out on his own and went to Johnstown in 1869 at the age of 25 and established a glove business at 27 & 29 South Market Street (on the area that is now the empty lot next to the First Presbyterian Church of Johnstown and the parking lot that sits behind the Frontier Telephone office on South William Street). This business eventually joined forces with his Father and Uncle's operation and became the nucleus of one of the largest glove manufacturing companies in the country.

Through his interest in the glove industry, he became a very keen student on tariffs and advocated for tariffs to tax imports of gloves made outside of the United States. While this was self-serving in that it protected his family's glove making enterprise, it also served to protect the same interests of many other United States manufactured products. Through this process he became one of the best posted men in the country on the subject of tariffs and their effects on Government revenues and the effects on the US Economy. This knowledge led to him often being summonsed to Washington, where his expert opinion was sought by the committees presenting/deciding on new tariffs.

In 1897, the Dingley Act was introduced by U.S. Representative Nelson Dingley, Jr. of Maine and brought protectionism to US manufacturing, as it imposed duties on many products and raw materials which had been duty-free since 1872. Northrup was an integral part in researching and making recommendations for the bill's provisions. He made it a point that "gloves" and the materials to make gloves were added to the list of items subject to the new import taxes that became incorporated into the bill. The hides being brought in to make gloves received up to a 20 per centum ad valorem, while finished gloves received duties of $1.75 to $4.50 per dozen pairs. Of the many of duties/tariffs that have been in place in the United States over its history, this act not only put a tax of 52% on certain imported products (the highest in history), but also lasted longer than any other tariff, 12 years. These tariffs and duties were instrumental in protecting the economy of Fulton County and allowing it to become the world leader in glove making.

Outside of work, Northrup was also very interested in the welfare of the community and anything that would improve the lives of those who worked for his family's company, as well as those throughout the Fulton County area. He was a trustee of the Glove Manufacturers Association, the Johnstown School Board, the Johnstown Library, the Humane Society and the Caroga Lake Protective Association. He even had a lake named after him – Northrup Lake. While hiking with a group of younger men in the late 1880's, they stumbled across an unnamed body of water about 3 miles west of Canada Lake. Since it had no name, the group decided that they should name it. And with that, they decided to name it after Northrup, as he was the eldest member of the group. To this day, the lake still carries his name (look at any government issued map, and you will find the lake just to the West of Canada Lake).

Northrup also had one other great love - the game of baseball. He was a devoted admirer of the sport and attended many local games. He also had a bad heart and despite his doctor's warning not to get "too excited", he just could not resist a good game of baseball. On June 4, 1908, he attended a New York State League professional game of baseball between the A., J. & G's (JAGS) and Syracuse at A., J. & G Park (Parkhurst Field) just a few miles up the road on Harrison Street in Gloversville. It was a very closely played game and once the JAGS took the lead in the 8th inning during some intense play, Northrup got too excited and was stricken with a heart attack and collapsed. Despite the efforts of three physicians (also attending the game) who worked on him for 30 minutes, he passed away at age of 63.

Ten months later, the Dingley Act, which had been the longest untouched tariff in the United States history, was replaced by the Payne-Aldrich Tariff on April 9, 1909. Without Northrup's input as to the effects of changes to the tariff rates, many items once protected by the Dingley Act saw drops in the rates initially set up to protect Fulton County industry. The tax rates on raw materials used to make gloves dropped in half, and the duties paid on finished gloves immediately dropped by $1 per dozen pairs. The Underwood-Simmons Tariff of 1913 saw key glove making raw materials added to the "Duty Free List", while the Fordney-McCumber Tariff of 1922 brought the addition of finished gloves added to the "Duty Free List". While the Hawley-Smoot Tariff of 1930 reestablished moderate tariffs and duties on the items key to protecting Fulton Counties economy, the leak of the Upstate New York manufacturers stronghold on the leather & glove markets following the death of Northrup had already taken its toll on the areas local economy and was a factor in its gradual decline.

Today, the game of baseball and the same park that Northrup succumbed to a heart attack at 110 years ago is at the center of plans to help rejuvenate the economy of Fulton County. Given Parkhurst Field's (A., J. & G Park) rich history of professional, semi-professional, world famous exhibition and youth baseball, combined with its proximity to Cooperstown, plans are being made to re-develop the park as a baseball destination and an ongoing economic revitalization diamond for the region. It is expected that a prominent baseball complex will draw Little League and travel baseball teams from around country for tournaments during the months that the Gloversville Little League season is not in operation (July & August). With these visiting teams will come revenue to benefit the local Little League, as well as tourism revenue to benefit the rest of the region. To learn more about the revitalization plans for the park and Fulton County's economy, visit www.parkhurstfield.org

M. Sexton Northrup.

89

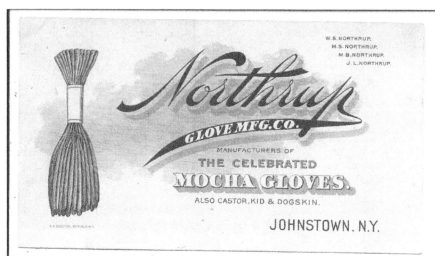

Northtrup Glove mfg. business card 1880s.

Northrup Building Brick Drawing.

70th Anniversary of Fredericks' season with the Glovers

From 1937 through 1951, the baseball fans of Fulton County were treated to professional baseball via the Class C Canadian-American League Gloversville-Johnstown Glovers. Their games took place at Berkshire Park (later to be called Glovers Park), which is the area now comprised of Runnings Outdoor Store, Hannaford Grocery Store and the House of Pizza Restaurant that make up the corner of Route 30A and Fifth Avenue in Gloversville. The Glovers were initially a minor league affiliate of the Brooklyn Dodgers in 1939, and from 1942-49 held an affiliation with the St. Louis Browns Major League Club of the American League.

Through their affiliation with the St. Louis Browns, the 1948 season was one that was extra special to the fans of Gloversville and Johnstown, as they got to root for a few home town boys as well as be treated to a visit from a Major League team.

The Glovers hometown connection began early in the season when they signed 1942 Johnstown High School graduate Charlie Fredericks to pitch for them. Fredericks, a 5-11 southpaw, was a standout First Baseman for Professor Wright's successful Johnstown teams of the early 1940's. Because of his strong throwing arm, he was converted into a pitcher while in high school. After high school, he attended Parks College of Engineering, Aviation and Technology in St. Louis Missouri where he continued to play at the college level. And during the summers, he was a star Pitcher in the Bi-County semi-professional league, pitching for local coaching legend Hank Cerrone on the Rhinehart A.C.'s of Johnstown. According to Fredericks' wife, Mary Jane, "whenever he was home from college, Uncle Hank (Cerrone) would recruit Charlie to pitch for him." It was during his summers pitching for Cerrone that he started to catch the attention of major league teams and local games would often have scouts from the New York Giants and Brooklyn Dodgers in the stands on nights he pitched. Instead of signing to play professionally, Fredericks opted to voluntarily enlist in the Navy on September 5, 1944 to serve his country in WWII. The afternoon before he left for basic training, he pitched for the A.C.'s against the St. Johnsville Nine and cruised to an easy complete game victory at Briggs Field in Johnstown. In his final at bat of the game, the contest was stopped, and to show their appreciation for his contributions to the team, he was given a purse of money that was taken up by teammates and fans as a thank you for his playing prowess and his upcoming military service. He then preceded to lay down a perfect bunt that he beat out for a single as the crowd cheered wildly. One day later he would officially enlist at the U.S. Naval Reserve Base in Springfield Missouri. He was eventually deployed to Naval Station Pearl Harbor in Hawaii as an Aviation Technician utilizing his education in Aeronautical Engineering.

Upon being honorably discharged from the Navy in 1946, he returned to Johnstown and once again suited up to pitch for Hank Cerrone teams for the summer. In addition to the Dodgers and Giants resuming their quest to sign him, the St. Louis Browns began to take notice of his pitching prowess. After a June 1947 game against Dolgeville at Hilltop Park in Dolgeville, in which he pitched a complete game 1 hitter, striking out 14 and going 2-2 at the plate, the St. Louis Browns offered him a contract to pitch professionally. According to Mary Jane, "Charlie always loved the Giants and had dreamed of one day playing for them. But, the Brown's beat both the Giants and the Dodgers to him." He signed with the Browns and was sent to their Class C Central Association League team in Hannibal Missouri. With the Hannibal Pilots, Fredericks compiled a 7-4 record and was a teammate of a 20-year old rookie by the name of Roy Sievers. Two seasons later, Sievers would make his Major League debut with the St. Louis Browns and win the American League Rookie of the Year for 1949. Sievers also would become a 5-time Major League Baseball All-Star, in a career that spanned from 1949 through 1965.

After starting the 1947 campaign back with Hannibal club, the St. Louis Browns organization transferred Fredericks to the "pitching starved" Gloversville-Johnstown Glovers for the 1948 season. This suited Fredericks very well, as he got to pitch in front of his hometown friends and family, as well as spend time with his future wife Mary Jane Peris of Johnstown. Many of you probably remember her as Madame Fredericks, who was a French Teacher at Gloversville High School from 1967 to 1988. This marked just the second time that an area boy would suit up for the Glovers since 1940 Johnstown High School graduate Eddie Zilka played for them in 1942.

Area fans got another thrill that season when the Glovers Major League parent club St. Louis Brown's came to Glovers Park to play them in an exhibition game on Tuesday July 13th. The Major League club participated in the 7th Annual Hall of Fame Game at Doubleday Field in Cooperstown the day before against the Philadelphia Phillies. After beating the Phillies by a score of 7-5, the team spent the night in Cooperstown and then traveled north to Fulton County the next day for an evening game in Gloversville. A pre-game reception for both teams and the media took place at the Pine Brook Golf Course on South Main Street in Gloversville. Each player received a pair of Gloversville made leather gloves from team president Bob Rothschild. The parent club of big leaguers beat the local team by a score of 24-11, and pounded out 26 hits, with five of them being home runs. Second baseman Andy Anderson hit three, and center fielder Pete Layden hit two. The 3,600 fans in attendance received another treat that day when 18-year old Gloversville resident Loren Stewart was put into the game to pitch in the fifth inning. Stewart, who had just graduated from Gloversville High School three weeks earlier, had recently signed a professional contact with the St. Louis Brown's. While he was not scheduled to report to play for the organization until the following spring, since the team was in his backyard, he was assigned to the Glovers for the day. The first pitch he threw as a professional player would be to a Major Leaguer (Pete Layden). As the 3,600 fans in the stands gave the local pitcher a standing ovation, Layden proceeded to deposit his very first offering over the left field fence for a home run. Stewart quickly settled down and ended up pitching three innings during the game. While he had not expected to start his career until the following spring, his performance that day earned him a spot as a starting pitcher on the Browns' "Stars of Tomorrow" squad, which was a touring group of the organization's top prospects who played charity fund raising games against all-star amateur teams across the country. He would eventually return to pitch full time for the Glovers for the 1950 and 1951 seasons.

Fredericks did not pitch in the exhibition game as the Glovers were in the hunt for the 1948 Canadian-American League Championship and they purposely "saved" him for games just before and just after that contest, which would help them in the standings.

The 1948 season also brought local baseball fans the opportunity to see future Major League Player/Manager and Hall of Famer Tommy Lasorda. The 20-year old Lasorda spent part of the season as a pitcher for Lee Riley's (Basketball Hall of Famer Pat Riley's father) Schenectady Blue Jays and first became famous for setting the then professional baseball record by striking out 25 batters in a 15-inning game against the Amsterdam Rugmakers. During the first half of a July 24th doubleheader between the Glovers and the Blue Jays at McNearney Stadium in Schenectady, both Fredericks and LaSorda were used as relief pitchers in the game. Lasorda also batted and hit the centerfield wall for a double, but it was not until later in that inning that Fredericks was brought in to relieve. They always seemed to be starting pitchers on opposite ends of doubleheaders or in games as relievers and never faced one another.

Transferring Fredericks to Gloversville would prove to be a wise decision by the Browns organization, as he was a great ticket draw and compiled a season record of 10-8. As a fan favorite, he often times earned a pair of "Gloversville made Gloves" whenever he had a good outing on the mound.

While he was offered a contract by the Browns to return for the 1949 season, Fredericks chose to retire from professional baseball so he could put his degree in aeronautical engineering to use and began working for General Electric in Schenectady. On July 9, 1949, he married Mary Jane Peris, and they started a family in 1951 that would include four daughters; Lynn, Terry, Jan and Marcia. Many of you know his youngest daughter as Marcia Gillis, who has been a Social Studies Teacher at the Gloversville Middle School since 2004. His career as an Engineer would take he and his family to jobs in California and Delaware. The family would return to Fulton County in 1957, where he would work for various area engineering firms and was a member of the American Society of Electrical Engineers. Fredericks converted to Catholicism after his marriage and was very active with St. Mary's Church in Gloversville. He was also a 3rd Degree Member of the Knights of Columbus Council #265 in Gloversville, where he served as the Council's Grand Knight from 1963 to 1965. Fredericks passed away in 1982 at the age of 57.

Fredericks' Johnstown made Denkert Baseball Glove that he used during his entire semi-professional and professional baseball career is on display at the Fulton County Museum in their "History of Fulton County Baseball Timeline Exhibit". Fredericks was inducted into the Fulton County Baseball & Sports Hall of Fame on August 11, 2018 at Parkhurst Field in Gloversville. The induction took place between innings of a Vintage Baseball Game between the A., J. & G's and the Mountain Athletic Club from Fleischmann's New York using 1895 style baseball rules and era authentic equipment.

Charles Fredericks Senior Picture, Johnstown, NY Class of 1942

Charles Fredericks with The Hannibal Pilots in 1947.
Fredericks is 2nd from the right.

1948 Gloversville Glovers team picture. Fredericks is sitting 3rd from the right.

Musillo joins Hall of Fame

From the 1920's through the 1960's, if you played football or baseball for the Gloversville High School program, you were under the guidance of Lawrence "Duke" Miller. Miller not only put winning teams on the field for both sports, he also had a knack for producing professional baseball players. In addition to Jack Sanford (1951) and Tom Foster (1953), he also helped produce a special player by the name of John "Chick" Musillo. Musillo was a four-sport standout at Gloversville for both Miller (football/baseball) and Jack Kobuskie (golf/basketball) where he was Coach K's sharp-shooter.

During his senior year at Gloversville High School, Musillo was highly sought after by college programs throughout the Northeast for basketball and baseball. This included Syracuse University, where he spent a weekend there being shown around campus by legendary coach Ben Schwartzwalder (featured in the Ernie Davis movie "The Express"). Upon graduating from high school in the spring of 1958, former Gloversville Glover (and Fulton County Sports Hall of Famer) John Coakley, who for many years was a scout for the Washington Senators, tried to sign Musillo to play professionally as a shortstop. However, Musillo's parents would not allow it, urging the 17-year old to instead attend college. Musillo would ultimately attend Ithaca College in the fall of 1958 to play baseball.

Over the next few summers, he played for local semi-professional teams including the Gloversville Merchants, Johnstown Tryon A.C.'s, Fulton County Glovers, Amsterdam Collegians and the Amsterdam Rug Makers. During his first summer after college baseball, Musillo took up pitching and became a star both on the mound and at the plate on every team he played on. Games in which he pitched drew the attention of scouts from the Cleveland Indians, Philadelphia Phillies, Milwaukee Braves, Kansas City Athletics, Los Angeles Dodgers, Boston Red Sox and St. Louis Cardinals.

In May of 1959, as a fundraiser to help finance the Amsterdam Collegians season, Baseball Hall of Fame Pitcher Satchel Paige and the Havana Cuban Stars came to Mohawk Mills Park (Shuttleworth Park) in Amsterdam to play an exhibition game against the Collegians. The Cuban Stars won the game 8-1, and Musillo went 3-4 and scored the Collegians only run with a Home Run. Also participating in that game were Fulton County players Babe Baldwin,

Zeke Zilka and Bob Manno.   After his performance in this game, Musillo was invited to Yankee Stadium for a tryout by the Cleveland Indians who were in New York for a series against the New York Yankees. During the tryout, he took grounders at third base hit by Hall of Famer Joe Gordon. Gordon, the Cleveland Manager at the time, was a 9-time American League All-Star, 5-time World Series Champion, and 1942 American League Most Valuable Player with the New York Yankees. When the Yankees took to the field for batting practice, Gordon brought Musillo to the sidelines to watch him throw. According to Musillo, "it was a thrill just to be on the field at Yankee Stadium. And when I glanced over at the batting cage, I noticed that Mickey Mantle was leaning on the cage watching me throw as he waited his turn to bat."

The 1960 summer season saw Musillo back in Amsterdam playing for the Rug Makers of the Schenectady Twilight League. Mid-season, he would be the both the starting and winning pitcher in the Twilight League All-Star Game. He would also pitch in another notable game that summer when he faced the New York Yankees Rookie Team. This team was sponsored by the New York Yankees to scout the New York City areas best prospects who had finished high school, but had not yet attended college or signed professionally.   The team barnstormed around the New England States and Quebec playing amateur and semi-professional teams. While the Rug Makers lost the game 6-4, Musillo went the distance and struck out 7 Yankees. These two performances upped his stock and he was signed by the St. Louis Cardinals that August at the age of 19.

Musillo finished out the 1960 season with the Rug Makers and reported to Homestead FL in the spring of 1961 for spring training with the St. Louis Cardinals. When spring training ended, the Cardinals sent him to the Billings Mustangs (Billings, MO) of the Class C Pioneer League. There, he appeared in 10 games, threw one complete game and compiled a record of 2-3. Mid-season, he was transferred to the Johnson City Cardinals (Johnson City, TN) of the Class D Appalachian League. He appeared in 22 more games, striking out 63 batters in 60 innings, and once again compiled a record of 2-3. That offseason, Musillo was offered a contract to play professional basketball for the Canadian Road Kings. The offer was for $350 per game, with a guarantee of 5-7 games per week. Not wanting to risk injury to his ankles, Musillo turned down the contract so he could focus on returning to baseball healthy the following spring.

During spring training going into the 1962 season, Musillo was with the Cardinals AAA team and his catcher was prospect Tim McCarver. McCarver would go on to play 21 seasons in the Major Leagues, and was a 2-time All-Star, 2-time World Series Champion (1964 & 1967 with the Cardinals), and a long-time Major League Baseball broadcaster (and Ford C. Frick Winner-Cooperstown HOF Broadcasters Wing). The 1962 regular season saw Musillo with the Brunswick Cardinals (Brunswick, GA) of the Class D Georgia-Florida League. He went 0-2 that season, appearing in 13 games and struck out 22 in 18 innings.

Musillo was released by the Cardinals after the 1962 season and went to spring training in 1963 with the Milwaukee Braves. His time with that organization was cut short when he was called to take a physical for the Vietnam War draft. During that physical, doctors discovered that he had a heart murmur and he was not drafted. He instead returned to Gloversville and resumed playing with the Polish American Veterans (P.A.V.) in the Schenectady Twilight League. During his time with the P.A.V. team (1963 to 1966), they won 4 league championships and 3 New York State Semi-Pro state championships.

In 1963 he married Rose Cristiano, and they would raise three children; Gregory, Dean and Kristin. He would spend his post-baseball career working for Levor & Company, Coca-Cola and Pearl Leather until his retirement in 2009. Musillo would continue to stay active on the local sports scene through the 1970's playing softball, basketball and golf in local Fulton County leagues.

Musillo was inducted into the Fulton County Baseball & Sports Hall of Fame on August 11, 2018 at Parkhurst Field in Gloversville. The induction took place between innings of a Vintage Baseball Game between the A., J. & G's and the Mountain Athletic Club from Fleischmann's New York using 1895 style baseball rules and era authentic equipment.

Chick Musillo in 1960 at Yankee Stadium in Dugout.

Chick Musillo in 1960 at Yankee Stadium in Dugout.

*Chick Musillo in 1960 at Yankee Stadium
with Indians Mgr. Joe Gordon
and coach Mel Harder*

Chick Musillo Pro Signing Announcement. Cartoon by Bob Luey.
Originally published in The Leader-Herald Newspaper
on August 13, 1960.

Baseball's Clown Prince appears in Gloversville

30 years-ago this summer (2018), Orion Pictures and writer/director Ron Shelton released the blockbuster baseball movie called 'Bull Durham'. The movie is a comedy that centers around a 12-year minor league baseball player who is sent down to the Durham Bulls of the Carolina League single-A level of professional baseball. The purpose of his demotion is to groom a hotshot rookie pitcher who is destined for greatness, but needs some mentoring. Their relationship is an intense one, and to add to their issues is a love interest they both have with a local "baseball groupie" which leads to an altercation at a local bar after a game. The movie features well-known Hollywood actors such as Kevin Costner (Crash Davis), Susan Sarandon (Annie Savoy), Tim Robbins (Ebby Calvin 'Nuke' LaLoosh) and Robert Wuhl (coach Larry Hockett). Also holding roles in the movie are former minor league players turned comedians Danny Gans and Max Patkin.

If you ever visited the Las Vegas strip between 1996 and 2009, chances are you saw the largest freestanding marquee in the world that advertised Gans comedy and vocal impressionist show that took place nightly at various hotels. In the movie, Gans played the Durham Bulls third baseman Deke. In real life, he was a minor league prospect in the Chicago White Sox organization until a leg injury ended his playing career. And if you frequented minor league ballparks from the late 1940's through the early 1990's, chances are you have seen the Clown Prince of Baseball Max Patkin perform his comedy routine. Patkin was also a minor league prospect who's playing career was derailed due to an injury. After professional baseball, Patkin joined the Navy during World War II. He was stationed in Hawaii, where he pitched for the Navy's service team. In a 1944 game against the Seventh Army Air Force Team, he faced New York Yankee legend Joe DiMaggio. DiMaggio homered off of Patkin, who in mock anger threw his glove down and then followed DiMaggio around the bases. The fans loved this comic relief and a new career was born for Patkin as a baseball comedian. After the war, he was hired by Hall of Fame owner Bill Veeck to be a base coach for the Cleveland Indians and to interject his comedy act into games for a few innings each night to entertain the fans. After Veeck sold the Indians in 1949, Patkin set out on his own and began barnstorming around the country putting on a vaudeville type comedy act as a base coach at minor league stadiums throughout the United States and

Canada. It is estimated that between 1944 and 1993 that he made over 4,000 appearances and logged over 100,000 miles per year.

In the movie, the entire Durham Bulls team ends up at a local bar after a game. Patkin (who plays himself) had just performed his comedy routine at that night's game and was sitting at a table in the bar sharing a drink with Annie Savoy (Sarandon). He then invites Crash Davis (Costner) over to their table and introduces them, setting off hostility between Davis and hot shot prospect Ebby Calvin 'Nuke" LaLoosh (Robbins), and an eventual love interest between Davis and Savoy. Patkin can be connected to Upstate New York through appearances he made at local ballparks over the years. From the 1950's through the 1980's, he made appearances in Albany, Schenectady, Glens Falls, Amsterdam, Little Falls and Utica. And on September 5, 1950, he brought his act of base coaching tricks to Glovers Park in Gloversville on the site that is now home to Runnings Outdoor, Hannaford Grocery and the House of Pizza Restaurant. Attendance for Glovers games had been slipping all season due to the popularity of television. This allowed baseball fans to stay home and watch Major League Games from the comfort of their own living rooms, leading to the eventual demise of minor league baseball in many cities in our area and across the country. In an attempt to boost attendance at the ballpark, Glovers President Bob Rothschild booked Patkin to perform at a game, making a promise that everyone attending would be treated to an enjoyable evening of clowning and fun showmanship. The night's game was played between the Gloversville Glovers and the Pittsfield Indians. Cold weather that evening limited attendance to 731 fans wearing winter coats in a game in which the Glovers lost 7-1. However, the fans in attendance were entertained with Patkin's variety of comical antics. His oversized uniform with a question mark in place of a uniform number, his hat on sideways and his pecking walk in which he looked like a long-necked crane drew laughs as he performed on the sidelines during the game. He also treated those in attendance to his telltale dance moves in which he danced the jitterbug, did imitations, twisted himself up like a pretzel and teased & frustrated the opposing pitcher and manager. Because Patkin's coaching-comedy act took place during the actual game, many old-school style managers did not appreciate Patkin's antics. According to longtime minor league & major league manager Jack McKeon (and 1950 Gloversville Glover who played in the Patkin game), "I managed many games in which Patkin performed. We actually became very good friends and he made me a part of his act in games we were both involved in". Whereas some managers did not like his act interfering with the flow of the game, McKeon embraced it. McKeon states "I simply went along with his act and anything he wanted to do in order to help him liven up the crowd. We often stayed in the same hotel on the road and he would always be at the bar dancing after games (similar to Robbin's 'Nuke' LaLoosh character in Bull Durham). Patkin and Jackie Price were two of the most entertaining performers who traveled the minor leagues and were fun to watch".

The next time you are watching the movie 'Bull Durham', be sure to take note of Patkin and his role in the film. And be certain to pay close attention to his comedy routine, as it is the same routine that he once performed right here in our own backyard. Future Upstate N.Y. Sports Lore columns will connect other iconic baseball movies to the Fulton County area. Such movies will include 'Field of Dreams', 'The Natural', 'The Pride of the Yankees', 'Eight Men Out' and 'The Sandlot'.

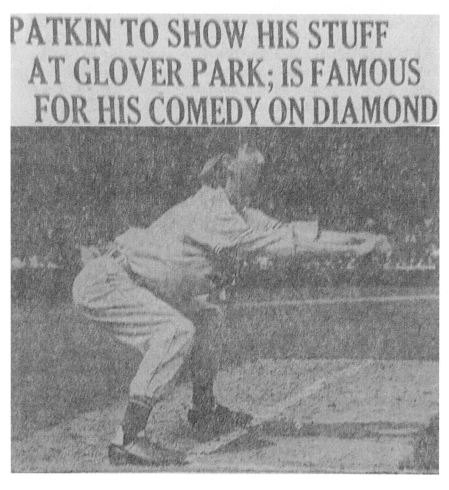

Max Patkin appears at Glovers Park.

The Undefeated GHS Maroon Nine:
Coach Duke Miller's pride and joy

From the 1920s through the 1960s, Gloversville High School coach Duke Miller produced numerous championship teams in both football and baseball. Along the way, he was also credited with producing future NFL star Dave Smukler (Philadelphia Eagles 1936-39) and numerous professional baseball players.

With all of Coach Miller's success over 40 years of coaching, the 1951 Gloversville High School varsity baseball team proved to be one that stood above all others. This is their story.

Due to a wet spring in 1951, Darling Field, located on Kingsboro Avenue, and the site of GHS baseball practices and games until the late 1970s was flooded. As a result of this, the 1951 baseball team was unable to practice outside. Many early season games were postponed and the team's first time on an outdoor field would be their opening game on April 20 in Wells, NY. Despite not having been outside all spring, they won that first game by a score of, 22-0.

The 1951 team then followed up that performance with 14-2 clubbing of the Mayfield Nine three days later at the Riceville Diamond in Mayfield. By May 4, 1951, Darling Field was finally game ready and they hosted the powerful Mont Pleasant Nine from Schenectady. The game went 13 innings, and with the score tied at 7-7 the contest was called due to darkness This would be the closest anyone would come to beating this team, as they went on to post wins in their next 13 games.

Over those 13 games, Gloversville scored 79 runs to their opponents 19 runs. This team was so respected across Upstate New York that the schools they had postponed early season games with, refused to make them up. This marked the first undefeated varsity baseball team in Gloversville's history. The next page presents a list of the 1951 GHS Maroon Nine, and features a brief biography on each player on the roster.

1951 Gloversville High School Varsity Baseball Team

Gene Satterlee

Pitcher (3-0) and outfielder, .500 batting average. Due to his incredible hitting, Miller was forced to put him in the outfield on days he was not pitching so he could bat. He would go on to play baseball at Cortland State and Springfield College. Many readers will remember Satterlee as a long-time physical education teacher and coach at   Gloversville Middle School and High School from the 1960s through the 1980s.

Don Shoblom

Right Field, .437 batting average. While the smallest player on the team, was a power hitter, with speed and a strong throwing arm.

Chuck Giardino

Catcher and outfielder, .436 batting average. Due to having to split catching time with Frank Ricco, Miller found playing time for him in the outfield due to his power hitting and base running abilities.

Jack Sanford (co-captain)

Pitcher (8-0), averaged 2 strikeouts per inning and walked fewer than two batters per game; threw four shutouts and had an ERA of 1.10 . He also had a season batting average of .433 . Many readers will remember him as a long-time physical education teacher and coach at Mayfield High School from the 1960s to the 1980s and a Flair's Gymnastics team coach.

Dick Grinnell

Pitcher (4-0), pitched six of the 13 innings in the game against Mont Pleasant. Had a season batting average of .400 .

Bob Richards

Center Field, .378 Batting Average. Possessed speed and a strong throwing arm in the outfield that cut-down runners trying to stretch extra base hits. Richards received a try-out with the Brooklyn Dodgers and would play many seasons in local semi-professional leagues after high school.

Dick LeFever

Third Base, .377 batting average. Great glove and strong throwing arm to first.

Joe Kobuskie (co-captain)

Shortstop, .362 batting average. Smooth fielder and accurate throwing arm to first. Many readers will remember Kobuskie as a long-time physical education Teacher and basketball coach at Oppenheim-Ephratah Junior/Senior High School.

John Recesso

Second Base, .351 batting average. Slick fielding second baseman, who along with LeFever, Kobuskie and DeLaurie made infield hits nearly impossible for the competition.

Frank Ricco

Catcher, .348 batting average. Defensive specialist at the catching position.

Larry "Bubbles" DeLaurie

First Base, .326 Batting Average. Great fielding first baseman.

Jim Meehan

Left Field, .319 Batting Average. Possessed great speed and a strong throwing arm.

Coaches/Managers

Lawrence "Duke" Miller (Head Coach)
Jack Kobuskie (Assistant Coach)
David Cornell (Team Manager)
Charles Catanzaro (Assistant Team Manager)
Bob Anderson (Assistant Team Manager)

This historic squad had a team batting average of .389 and consistently drew the attention of professional scouts. Six of their wins were shut outs, in which they out-scored their opponents 76-0.

Overall, they compiled a record of 15-0-1 and scored a total of 156 runs to their opponents 28. This marked the only undefeated varsity baseball team in Gloversville's history.

According to 1951 pitcher/outfielder Gene Satterlee, *"A perfect season in baseball is very unique. There are so many factors working against it; team hitting, team fielding, umpires calls, etc. An undefeated season is a true rarity, and I don't think we have seen such a season by any area teams since."*

Most of the members of this team would go on to play at the college or semi-professional level, and four players would be signed to play professionally.

Jack Sanford

Sanford went on to pitch for Springfield College (1953-55), where he was one of the most successful pitchers in college baseball during that span. Over three seasons, he compiled a 19-3 record and helped lead Springfield to the College World Series in Omaha, Neb., in 1955. After graduating from Springfield in 1955, he was signed to a professional contract with the Pittsburgh Pirates. He spent the 1955 and 1956 seasons with the Williamsport Grays (Williamsport, Pa.) of the Eastern League. In 1956, he was Williamsport's pitching work-horse, winning eight games, while appearing in 33 (23 starts and 10 relief appearances). He spent the 1957 season with the St. Louis Cardinals organization, pitching for the Jacksonville Braves (Jacksonville, Fla.) in the South Atlantic League. In 1958, he split time with the New York White Roses (York, Pa.) of the Eastern League and then back in the Pirates organization with the Lincoln Chiefs of the Western League in Lincoln, Neb.

Joe Kobuskie

Kobuskie would team up again with Jack Sanford at Springfield College for the 1954 and 1955 seasons. The two also spent the summer seasons playing for the Grand Falls Cataracts (Grand Falls, New Brunswick, Canada) in the Maine-New Brunswick League (a league similar to the Perfect Game League in which the Amsterdam Mohawks participate in). After competing in the College World Series with Springfield in 1955, Kobuskie was signed to play professionally by the Kansas City Athletics. The 1955 season saw him with the Savannah A's (Savannah, Ga.) in the Class A South Atlantic League. In 1956 he was signed by the Pittsburgh Pirates organization, and spent the season with the Class D Clinton Pirates (Clinton, Iowa) of the Midwest League.

Frank Ricco

Upon graduating high school in 1952, Ricco was signed by the New York Yankees as a catching prospect. He spent the 1952 and 1953 seasons with the Olean Yankees (Olean NY) in the Class D Pennsylvania-Ontario-New York League. He was the team's #1 catcher, batting .301 with 8 home runs in 1953, while developing the nickname "the Hustling Yankee" for his fielding prowess. In 1954 he split time with the St. Joseph Saints (St. Joseph MO) in the Class C Western Association and the McAlester Rockets (McAlester OK) in the Class D Sooner State League. In his last season (1955), he started the season with the Modesto Reds (Modesto CA) of the Class C California League. He would finish the season with the Bristol Twins (Bristol VA) of the Class D Appalachian League.

Don Shoblom

After graduating from Gloversville High School in the spring of 1951, Shoblom took a different route to professional baseball. He initially chose to join the Navy and served as a seaman aboard the carrier Saipan. After two years of service, he was honorably discharged in October of 1953. He then attended the Sid Hudson Baseball School in Kissimmee Florida and was instructed by Hudson (former Washington Senator and Boston Red Sox), future Hall of Famer Johnny Mize (former St. Louis Cardinal, New York Giant, New York Yankee), Ted Lepcio (Utica native & former Boston Red Sox), Mickey Vernon (14 year Major League career with 7 teams), Jimmy Piersall (16 year Major League career with 5 teams), and Dick Gernhert (10 year Major League career with 5 teams). Of the 35 players who were chosen to attend the school, only Shoblom and two other players were signed by Major League organizations to a professional contract at the end of the training. The Chicago White Sox signed Shoblom to a contract and he reported to San Angelo Texas in March of 1954. He spent the first part of the 1954 season with the San Angelo Colts of the Class C Appalachian League. Mid-season, he received an assignment to join the Pauls Valley Raiders (Pauls Valley OK) of the Class D Sooner State

League. While with Pauls Valley, he went up against former Gloversville High School teammate Frank Ricco, who was with the McAlester Rockets, who were also in the Sooner State League.

1951 Catcher/Outfielder Chuck Giardino fondly remembers that undefeated season and Coach Duke Miller. According to Giardino, *"Miller was not only a great coach, but he also deeply cared for all of his players. He was so proud of our team going undefeated, that he personally purchased a baseball figurine for each player as a keepsake remembrance of our undefeated season."*

For their accomplishment of being the only Varsity Baseball team in the history of Gloversville High School to complete an undefeated season, the entire 1951 GHS Varsity Baseball team was inducted into the Fulton County Baseball & Sports Hall of Fame on May 31, 2020. The inductions came during the annual Vintage Baseball Game at Parkhurst Field in Gloversville and marked the very first team to be enshrined.

For more information about the inductions and vintage game, visit www.parkhurstfield.org.

Author's Note: A special 'thank you' to Gene Satterlee, Jack and Diane Sanford, Tom Foster, Jennie Shoblom, Chuck Giardino, Garry Roorda and Springfield College archivist Jeffrey L. Monseau for their input in writing this story.

Gloversville High School's first undefeated team in history had the following leading roles:

Front row, left to right: John Recesso, second baseman; Dick LeFever, third baseman; Co-Captain Jack Sanford, pitcher: Larry "Bubbles" DeLaurie, first base; Co-Captain Joe Kobuskie, shortstop.

Second Row: L.A. "Duke" Miller, coach; Gene Satterlee, pitcher; Dick Grinnell, pitcher; Frank Recco, catcher; Chuck Giardino, catcher; David Cornell, manager.

Third Row: Charles Catanaro, assistant manager; Bob Richards, centerfield; Jim Meehan, leftfield; Don Shoblom, rightfield; Bob Anderson, assistant manager.

1951 Gloversville High School Baseball Team.

DON SHOMLOM SHOWS FRANK RICCO where he will be playing Class C baseball this year. Shoblom was signed recently by the Chicago White Sox to play with San Angelo, Tex., in the Longhorn League. Ricco, who played baseball with him at Gloversville High School several years ago, is under contract with the New York Yankees and expects to play this year either with Norfolk, Va., in the Class B Piedmont League or with Binghamton in the Class A Eastern League. He played with Olean in the Class D Pony circuit the last two seasons.

Jack Sanford and Joe Kobuskie & the Springfield Team boarding a plane to travel to Omaha Nebraska for the 1955 College World Series. They are in the row standing; 4th & 5th from the right.

1951 Gloversville High School Baseball teammates Gene Satterlee and Jack Sanford still gather for coffee every morning.

About The Author

Mike Hauser and his passion for sports history began when he was a young child listening to tales of the sports legends of the past as told to him by his maternal grandfather Earl Way. Luckily for Mike these sports history conversations with his grandfather lasted for over 40 years and he was always attentively listening and taking notes. In 1991, Mike began hosting the Twin Cities Sports Card & Memorabilia Show in Johnstown, New York. Through these events he began working relationships and friendships with many professional athletes, including some of the all-time greats of both baseball and football. In 2006, Mike expanded his sports knowledge and successful trade show experience by hosting the first Adirondack Outdoorsman Show, an event that is held every February in Johnstown, New York and caters to hunters, fisherman and outdoor enthusiasts (www.adkshow.com). Mike is the founder of the Fulton County Baseball & Sports Hall of Fame in Upstate New York (www.fchof.com), and he also serves as the Vice-President of the Parkhurst Field Foundation in Gloversville, New York. The foundations efforts include supporting the Gloversville Little League and revitalizing one of the oldest continuously used baseball grounds in the world. In his spare time Mike enjoys researching and documenting Upstate New York's rich and fascinating sports history, fishing with his family & friends, and traveling with his wife Lori. Mike currently lives in beautiful upstate New York in the foothills of the Adirondack Mountains. To follow Mike and his sports writing news and announcements, like him on Facebook by searching for "Mike Hauser - Author".

A Note from Mike...

Thank you for reading this book! If you have feedback or questions, I would enjoy hearing from you. Also, if you have any ideas for future sports stories or athletes who are "Hometown Sports Heroes" that would make a good article in a future addition to this series, feel free to contact me at the email address below, or by Facebook Messenger at "Mike Hauser –Author". Thanks again!

Sincerely,
Mike Hauser
Gloversville, NY
mhauser@frontiernet.net

Also by Mike Hauser:

Check out Mike's Baseball and Football e-books on amazon.com
Search for "Hometown Sports Heroes"

END NOTES

1. "Victor Hugo." *Wikipedia.com,* 23 March 2019. en.wikipedia.org/wiki/Victor_Hugo

2. Ries, Al and Jack Trout. <u>Positioning: The battle for your mind.</u> McGraw-Hill Education. 2001. Pages 189, 193.

3. "Parkhurst Field Foundation." *Parkhurstfield.org,* 23 March 2019. parkhurstfield.org/

4. Hauser, Mike. Hometown Sports Heroes: Book 3 Classic Baseball Tales. Great Point Publishing. 2019.

5. "The beginning of JAGS baseball." *Parkhurstfield.org,* 23 March 2019. parkhurstfield.org/the-beginning-of-jags-baseball/

6. "New Clubhouse Planned." *Parkhurstfield.org,* 23 March 2019. parkhurstfield.org/new-clubhouse-planned/

7. "Samuel I. Lucas, Supervisor of Darling Field and Littauer Pool 25 Years, Dies Suddenly." *The Leader-Republican,* Gloversville and Johnstown, NY. 20 March 1948. Page 12.

8. "Baseball Diamond Location." *Parkhurstfield.org,* 23 March 2019. parkhurstfield.org/baseball-diamond/

9. Francis, Bill. "At Home on the Road." *baseballhall.org,* 23 March 2019. baseballhall.org/discover-more/history/barnstorming-tours

10. "Positioning (marketing)." *Wikipedia.com,* 23 March 2019. en.wikipedia.org/wiki/Positioning_(marketing)

11. Hauser, Mike. Hometown Sports Heroes: Book 1 Classic Baseball Tales. Great Point Publishing. 2019.

12. "Chief Bender plays AJG Park." *Parkhurstfield.org,* 23 March 2019. parkhurstfield.org/chief-bender-plays-a-j-g-park/

13. Miller, Sam. "The Home Run Derby and The Beauty of Baseball that Doesn't Count." *espn.com*, 23 March 2019. espn.com/mlb/story/_/id/24101014/mlb-home-run-derby-beauty-baseball-count

14. Fay, John and Jeff Suess. "Chuck Harmon, the Reds' first African-American player, has died at the age of 94." *cincinnati.com*, 24 March 2019. cincinnati.com/story/sports/mlb/reds/2019/03/20/chuck-harmon-first-aftican-american-cincinnati-reds-dead-94/3222687002/

15. Fox, Kirk. "Notable Deaths. Chuck Harmon (1924–2019), first African-American to play for the Cincinnati Reds." *legacy.com*, 24 March 2019. legacy.com/news/celebrity-deaths/notable-deaths/article/chuck-harmon-1924-2019-first-african-american-to-play

Previous versions of Hauser's articles can also be found at:

A version of "Russell Holmes – Gloversville's Fenway Park Connection" was originally published on May 1, 2016 in the Leader-Herald Newspaper.

A version of "Grimshaw brings the big leagues, Cy Young to Gloversville" was originally published on June 5, 2016 in the Leader-Herald Newspaper.

A version of "Schumacher - Upstate New York's Prince of Baseball" was originally published on July 3, 2016 in the Leader-Herald Newspaper.

A version of "Chickens, Tigers & Pirates...Mayfield Baseball of course" was originally published on August 7, 2016 in the Leader-Herald Newspaper.

A version of "Jack McKeon...Back to his Gloversville Roots" was originally published on September 4, 2016 in the Leader-Herald Newspaper.

A version of "Pittsburgh Pirates once visited Gloversville's Berkshire Park" was originally published on June 4, 2017 in the Leader-Herald Newspaper.

A version of "The Integration of Professional Baseball had roots in Fulton County" was originally published on May 7, 2018 in the Leader-Herald Newspaper.

A version of "110th Anniversary of the Greatest Month in Gloversville Baseball History" was originally published on July 2, 2017 in the Leader-Herald Newspaper.

A version of "Vintage Baseball in Fulton County" was originally published on August 6, 2017 in the Leader-Herald Newspaper.

A version of "Generations mirror each other at Parkhurst Field" was originally published on September 3, 2017 in the Leader-Herald Newspaper.

A version of "Foster, Sanford and baseball with a Flair" was originally published on April 8, 2018 in the Leader-Herald Newspaper.

A version of "The Death & Rebirth of an economy at the Ballpark" was originally published on June 9, 2018 in the Leader-Herald Newspaper.

A version of "70th Anniversary of Frederick's season with the Glovers" was originally published on July 1, 2018 in the Leader-Herald Newspaper.

A version of "Musillo joins Hall of Fame" was originally published on August 5, 2018 in the Leader-Herald Newspaper.

A version of "Baseball's Clown Prince appears in Gloversville" was originally published on September 2, 2018 in the Leader-Herald Newspaper.

A version of "The Undefeated GHS Maroon Nine: Coach Duke Miller's pride and joy" was originally published on November 9, 2019 in the Leader-Herald Newspaper.

Made in the USA
Middletown, DE
29 November 2019